ChemLab

METALS

Grolier Educational
SHERMAN TURNPIKE, DANBURY, CONNECTICUT 06816

First published in the United States in 1998
by Grolier Educational, Sherman Turnpike,
Danbury, CT 06816

Copyright © 1998
Atlantic Europe Publishing Company Limited

Author
Brian Knapp, BSc, PhD
Project consultant
*Keith B. Walshaw, MA, BSc, DPhil
(Head of Chemistry, Leighton Park School)*
Project Director
Duncan McCrae, BSc
Editor
Mary Sanders, BSc
Special photography
Ian Gledhill
Illustrations
The Ascenders Partnership, David Woodroffe
Electronic page makeup
The Ascenders Partnership
Designed and produced by
EARTHSCAPE EDITIONS
Print consultants
Chromo Litho Ltd
Reproduced in Malaysia by
Global Colour
Printed and bound in Italy by
L.E.G.O. SpA

Library of Congress Cataloging-in-Publication Data
ChemLab
    p. cm.
    Includes indexes.
    Contents: v.1.Gases, liquids, and solids –
v.2.Elements, compounds, and mixtures – v.3.The
periodic table – v.4.Metals – v.5.Acids, bases, and salts
– v.6.Heat and combustion – v.7.Oxidation and
reduction – v.8.Air and water chemistry – v.9.Carbon
chemistry – v.10.Energy and chemical change –
v.11.Preparations – v.12. Tests.
    ISBN 0–7172–9146–4 (set). – ISBN 0–7172–9150–2 (v.4).
    1. Chemistry – Juvenile literature. [1. Chemistry.]
I. Grolier Educational (Firm)
QD35.C52 1997
540–dc21   97–23250
                                                CIP
                                                AC

Picture credits
All photographs are from the **Earthscape
Editions** photolibrary except the
following:
(c=center t=top b=bottom l=left r=right)
Mary Evans Picture Library 6tr, 7tr

*This product is manufactured from sustainable
managed forests. For every tree cut down at
least one more is planted.*

Contents

HOW TO USE THIS BOOK

These two pages show you how to get the most from this book.

❶ THE CONTENTS

Use the table of contents to see how this book is divided into themes. Each theme may have one or more demonstrations.

❷ THEMES

Each theme begins with a theory section on yellow-colored paper. Major themes may contain several pages of theory for the demonstrations that are presented on the subsequent pages. They also contain biographies of scientists whose work was important in the understanding of the theme.

❸ DEMONSTRATIONS

Demonstrations are at the heart of any chemistry study. However, many demonstrations cannot easily be shown to a whole class for health and safety reasons, because the demonstration requires a closeup view, because it is over too quickly, takes too long to complete, or because it requires special apparatus. The demonstrations shown here have been photographed especially to overcome these problems and give you a very closeup view of the key stages in each reaction.

The text, pictures, and diagrams are closely connected. To get the best from the demonstration, look closely at each picture as soon as its reference occurs in the text.

Many of the pictures show enlarged views of parts of the demonstration to help you see exactly what is happening. Notice, too, that most pictures form part of a sequence. You will find that it pays to look at the picture sequence more than once, and always be careful to make sure you can see exactly what is described in any picture before you move on.

The main heading for a demonstration or a set of demonstrations.

An introduction expands on the heading, summarizing the demonstration or group of demonstrations and their context in the theme.

Each demonstration is carefully explained and illustrated with photographs and, where necessary, with diagrams, tables, and graphs. The illustrations referred to are numbered ①, ②, ③, etc.

Chemical equations are shown where appropriate (see the explanation of equations at the bottom of page 5).

The photographs show the key stages that you might see if witnessing a demonstration firsthand. Examine them very carefully against the text description.

APPARATUS

The demonstrations have been carefully conducted as representative examples of the main chemical processes. The apparatus used is standard; but other choices are possible, and you may see different equipment in your laboratory. So make sure you understand the principles behind the apparatus selected. The key pieces of apparatus are defined in the glossary.

❹ GLOSSARY OF TECHNICAL TERMS

Words with which you may be unfamiliar are shown in small capitals where they first occur in the text. Use the glossary on pages 66–74 to find more information about these technical words. Over four hundred items are presented alphabetically.

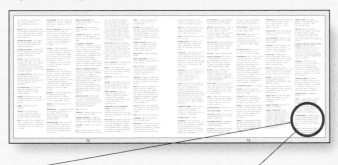

❺ INDEX TO ALL VOLUMES IN THE SET

To look for key words in any of the 12 volumes that make up the ChemLab set, use the Master Index on pages 75 to 80. The instructions on page 75 show you how to cross-reference between volumes.

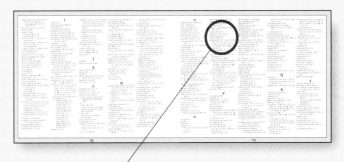

The most important locations of the term "oxidizing agent" are given in a master index that includes references to all of the volumes in the ChemLab set.

oxidizing agent: a substance that removes electrons from another substance being oxidized (and therefore is itself reduced) in a redox reaction. *Example:* chlorine (Cl_2).

ABBREVIATIONS

Units are in the international metric system. Some units of measurement are abbreviated, or shortened, as follows:
°C = degrees Celsius
km = kilometer
m = meter
cm = centimeter
mm = millimeter
sq m = square meter
g = gram
kg = kilogram
kJ = kilojoule
l = liter

❻ CHEMICAL EQUATIONS

Important or relevant chemical equations are shown in written and symbolic form along with additional information.

What the reaction equation illustrates

Word equation

Symbol equation
The symbols for each element can be found in any Periodic Table.

Where relevant, the oxidation state is shown as Roman numerals in parentheses.

EQUATION: Reaction of copper and nitric acid
Copper + nitric acid ⇨ copper(II) nitrate + water + nitrogen dioxide
$Cu(s) + 4HNO_3(conc) ⇨ Cu(NO_3)_2(aq) + 2H_2O(l) + 2NO_2(g)$
Blue

The symbol indicating the state of each substance is shown as follows:
(*s*) = solid
(*g*) = gaseous
(*l*) = liquid
(*aq*) = aqueous
(*conc*) = concentrated

The two halves of the chemical equation are separated by the arrow that shows the progression of the reaction. Each side of the equation must balance.

Sometimes additional descriptions are given below the symbol equation.

The correct number of atoms, ions, and molecules and their proportions in any compound are shown by the numbers. A free electron is shown as an e⁻.

INTRODUCTION

Metals make up three-quarters of all the ELEMENTS. They occur on the left-hand side of the Periodic Table (①, as distinct from nonmetals, which are found to the right).

Metals are characteristically shiny (they have what is known as a "metallic luster"). This is shown, for example, by the surface of a "silver mirror" precipitated on the inside of a flask (②).

Most metals are solids at room temperature and have high MELTING POINTS. The best known exception is mercury, which is a liquid at room temperature. Tungsten has the highest melting point of all the common metals at 3410°C (6170°F). Metals are also good conductors of electricity (③).

① The metals, semimetals (metalloids), and nonmetals

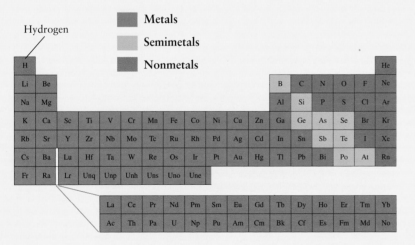

Hydrogen

Metals
Semimetals
Nonmetals

Sir Humphry Davy

Sir Humphry Davy (1778–1829) was a famous English chemist born in Cornwall and the first to discover many metals, including sodium and potassium. He also proved that chlorine and iodine were elements. In later life, he invented the miner's safety lamp.

Davy was educated as an apothecary (an early version of a pharmacist) and was self-educated in science. Davy was fascinated by the ideas of another famous scientist, Antoine Laurent Lavoisier, and he began to experiment with light and heat. In 1801 he was asked to become lecturer in chemistry at the newly founded Royal Institution of Great Britain in London. Over the following years Davy made some remarkable discoveries and was also a very popular lecturer. One of those who saw his lectures was Michael Faraday, who later became Davy's assistant before going on himself to be one of the greatest experimental scientists of all time.

Just a year before Davy was made lecturer in chemistry, Alessandro Volta in Italy made the world's first battery. This was used to dissociate water into oxygen and hydrogen, a process called ELECTROLYSIS. It was these two events that determined the path of Davy's investigations. In 1808 Davy isolated the metals sodium and potassium electrically. He later isolated calcium, strontium, barium, magnesium, and boron.

Davy's experiments on electrolysis led him to believe that electrolysis was caused by ions having opposite electrical charges. He went on to suggest that the tendency for metals to displace each other was related to their relative reactivity and so laid the foundation for the electrochemical series for metals.

Davy was able to use the principle of the electrochemical series to suggest the CATHODIC PROTECTION method of preventing the corrosion of ships' hulls.

②

Silver deposited on the inside of a round-bottomed flask

③

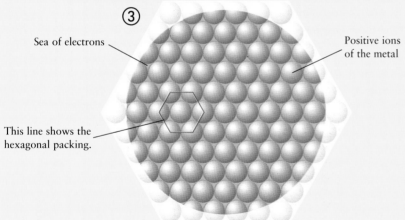

Sea of electrons

Positive ions of the metal

This line shows the hexagonal packing.

(Above) **A metal consists of closely packed positive IONS (CATIONS) embedded in a "sea" of ELECTRONS that bond the ions together. Every ion is surrounded by six others to produce a hexagonal (as above) or a cubical packing, and this gives metals their high densities. The strong bonds between the ions and the free electrons are responsible for the high melting points of metals and make them good conductors of heat and electricity.**

GREAT EXPERIMENTAL SCIENTISTS
Michael Faraday

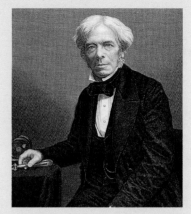

Michael Faraday (1791–1867) was a famous experimental scientist of the 19th century whose career began under the guidance of Sir Humphry Davy at the Royal Institution in London. While there (as well as many other achievements), he laid the foundations of the science of electrochemistry.

Faraday was unusual among early scientists in coming from a poor background and having received limited education. He was an apprentice to a bookbinder. He first saw Sir Humphry Davy at one of his public science lectures, and when the opportunity arose to become his assistant, his career had begun.

He was later made director of the Royal Institution's laboratory and professor of chemistry, but he declined all the public honors that he was offered.

Faraday worked on both chemical and physical problems. In the area of chemistry Faraday spent much time working with electrochemical reactions, and he formulated the first laws of electrolysis, also defining the terms electrode, anode, cathode, ion, anion, cation, ionization, electrolyte, and electrolysis. He suggested that, during electrolysis, positively charged cations move toward the negatively charged cathode, and negatively charged anions move toward the positively charged anode of a cell.

Faraday also demonstrated that a material could act as a catalyst, using platinum as his example.

Amazingly, Faraday achieved all of his great discoveries and set out his theories without any real ability in mathematics. He worked out everything in pictorial form.

The faraday (the quantity of electricity required to liberate a standard amount of a substance in electrolysis) is named in his honor.

All metals are CRYSTALLINE when solid, and most form cubes or hexagon shapes. However, in many cases the crystal structure of the metal depends on the temperature and pressure at which it was formed. This property is called POLYMORPHISM.

Metals are also MALLEABLE, which means they are not brittle and can be bent or hammered into shape. Metals lose their strength when heated about half-way toward their melting points because at this temperature the atoms have expanded apart so far that they are no longer locked together in a rigid way.

Because so many of the elements are metals, metals vary considerably in their properties. The most reactive metals (such as sodium and potassium) make up Group 1 of the Periodic Table (④). The Group 2 metals are slightly less reactive. This group includes calcium and magnesium. Many metals (including copper and iron) are TRANSITION METALS. These have a wide range of properties, but most noticeable is that they form highly colored COMPOUNDS. Metals in Group 3 are slightly less reactive than those in Group 2. Only two metals, tin and lead, are in Group 4, and the only metal in Group 5 is bismuth.

Many metals are also grouped together because they share similar properties. For example, the precious metals group includes silver, gold, and platinum. These share not only a rarity value, but they are also very unreactive (gold and platinum do not tarnish at all).

Some metals also share other important properties, such as being CATALYSTS for reactions. Platinum is a catalyst for carbon-based compounds, while manganese is a catalyst for the release of oxygen from hydrogen peroxide.

The outer electrons in metals are not firmly bound to individual atoms but can move relatively freely in the solid or liquid. It is this extraordinary feature that gives metals many of their unique properties, such as being able to conduct electricity. The resultant "core" of a metal atom is thus an ION with a positive charge. The atom is made electrically neutral by attracting sufficient electrons that are moving about freely within the metal.

Metal reactions

Chemical reactions occur when atoms exchange their outer electrons. Most metals have between one and three outer electrons (in contrast to the nonmetals,

④ **The metal blocks**

Groups 1 and 2 form one "block" in the Periodic Table

Transition metals make up a second "block" with their own characteristic properties.

H																	He
Li	Be											B	C	N	O	F	Ne
Na	Mg											Al	Si	P	S	Cl	Ar
K	Ca	Sc	Ti	V	Cr	Mn	Fe	Co	Ni	Cu	Zn	Ga	Ge	As	Se	Br	Kr
Rb	Sr	Y	Zr	Nb	Mo	Tc	Ru	Rh	Pd	Ag	Cd	In	Sn	Sb	Te	I	Xe
Cs	Ba	Lu	Hf	Ta	W	Re	Os	Ir	Pt	Au	Hg	Tl	Pb	Bi	Po	At	Rn
Fr	Ra	Lr	Unq	Unp	Unh	Uns	Uno	Une									

La	Ce	Pr	Nd	Pm	Sm	Eu	Gd	Tb	Dy	Ho	Er	Tm	Yb
Ac	Th	Pa	U	Np	Pu	Am	Cm	Bk	Cf	Es	Fm	Md	No

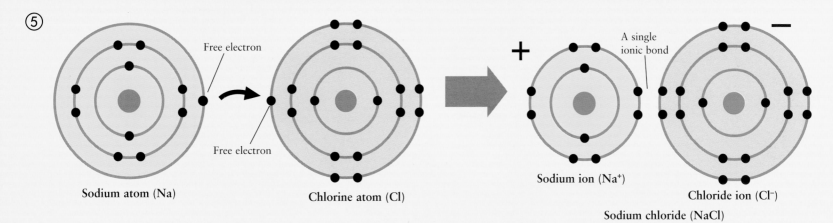

⑤

Free electron

Sodium atom (Na)

Free electron

Chlorine atom (Cl)

+

A single ionic bond

−

Sodium ion (Na⁺)

Chloride ion (Cl⁻)

Sodium chloride (NaCl)

(Right) **Crystalline rock salt is the ionic compound sodium chloride (NaCl).**

which have between five and eight outer electrons).
Metal elements with few outer electrons, e.g., sodium,
are very reactive chemically (as are nonmetals with
almost a complete set of outer electrons).

When, for example, the metal sodium and the
nonmetal chlorine react, the sodium gives up its single
outer electron (⑤) (but it keeps the remainder of its
inner electrons). It therefore becomes stable. Chlorine
(which has seven outer electrons), takes the electron
from sodium, giving it a full, and stable, complement
of eight outer electrons. As a result, the compound,
sodium chloride (common salt) is very stable (see
page 28).

No reaction can take place without a change of
energy. In the case of sodium and chlorine heat energy
has to be applied for the reaction to occur, but the
formation of a solid lattice of oppositely charged ions

then releases energy. So, overall, energy is given out
(it is an EXOTHERMIC reaction), and compounds of
metals have very strong BONDS (ionic bonds).

Crystals of sodium chloride are held together
entirely by a network of ionic bonds. However,
because the sodium electrons are now locked up
in the structure, the metal compound, unlike its
parent metal, cannot allow electrons to move freely,
and so it is an insulator. It has no ability to bend, and
so it is brittle.

Amalgams

An amalgam is an alloy of metals in which mercury is a component. Most common solid metals react with liquid mercury to form amalgams even at room temperature, although the reaction is greatly speeded up if the mercury is heated.

Demonstration: alloy-forming properties of mercury

The demonstration uses part of an aluminum pie dish and a piece of very thin aluminum foil. To make the amalgam, a compound of mercury (mercury(II) nitrate) is used rather than pure liquid mercury because of the dangers associated with inhaling the fumes given off by pure mercury.

To make an amalgam, the metal to be amalgamated with mercury has to be bright and clean and have no oxide coating. To ensure this, the metal surface must be cleaned either by scratching it with abrasive paper or by dipping it in dilute acid.

Here the surface of the aluminum is scratched using abrasive paper to reveal the pure metal, and the mercury nitrate is instantly applied (①), before the aluminum develops an oxide coating again.

When the mercury nitrate is placed on the aluminum, the reaction between the aluminum and the nitrate releases mercury, which then forms an amalgam with the aluminum (②). The process is exothermic, and so the aluminum gets hot during the reaction.

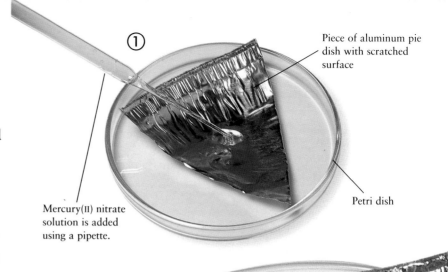

① Piece of aluminum pie dish with scratched surface

Mercury(II) nitrate solution is added using a pipette.

Petri dish

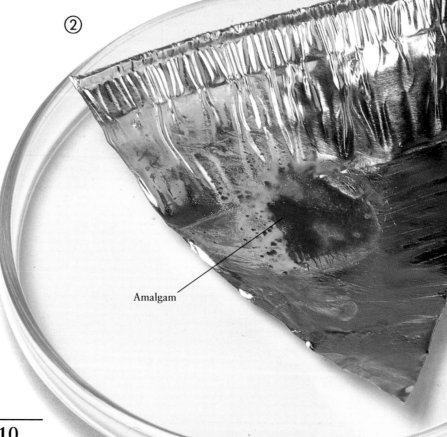

② Amalgam

If a thin aluminum foil is used instead of a thicker sheet from a dish, the result is to "pepper" the foil with holes (③). The foil is so much thinner than the dish that the aluminum is more easily removed.

Remarks

Because it is a liquid, mercury cannot develop a coating of unreactive oxide. Thus it is particularly reactive with other metals. This reaction involves the displacement of mercury from the nitrate to form pure liquid. This happens because aluminum is more reactive than mercury (see page 21).

③

Because the sheet is thin, all the aluminum mixes with the mercury at the places where the mercury droplets settle. The result is a pattern of holes where the aluminum has simply become part of the amalgam, which then falls away.

Metals reacting with air

Most metals rapidly OXIDIZE in air, causing them to tarnish. The most reactive metals also combust in air.

The most reactive metals are in Groups 1 and 2 of the Periodic Table. They have just one electron in their outer shell, and they readily give this up to an oxygen atom, which needs two electrons to make up its outer shell. This means that the sodium and oxygen easily react and produce a surface oxide — tarnishing.

Demonstration 1: sodium and air

Sodium is a very soft metal. Sodium (and similar metals such as potassium) will also react with water, which is why they are normally kept in an organic liquid such as hexane.

If a silvery pellet of sodium is cut while it is in hexane, the shiny cut surface is easy to see. If the sodium is cut on a bench surface in air (which must in any case be done quickly because of the chance of the sodium igniting), it tarnishes more quickly than the freshly cut surface can be exposed, and a fresh surface can never be seen.

②

③

The cut surface of the sodium pellet has a shiny surface that tarnishes very quickly.

①

Sodium pellet

Liquid hexane

EQUATION: Reaction of sodium metal in air
Sodium + oxygen in air ⇨ sodium oxide
$4Na(s) + O_2(g) \Rightarrow 2Na_2O(s)$

Demonstration 2: aluminum and air

Many metals that do not react violently when exposed to air still oxidize very quickly, but the extremely thin layer of oxide formed by the rapid reaction is transparent and so cannot be detected. Furthermore, it acts as a "sealant," preventing further reaction.

Aluminum, for example, appears unreactive because, as soon as new metal is exposed to air, it forms a very complete (known as COHERENT) oxide coating that then stops further reaction occurring.

If the aluminum can be exposed continuously to air, however, oxide is produced in great quantities.

This is most readily demonstrated by forming an amalgam of aluminum with mercury (see the amalgam demonstration, page 10). Because the aluminum is in a liquid alloy, it does not form a stable coating, and so the oxide continues to grow very rapidly. White aluminum oxide appears as a crust within a few minutes.

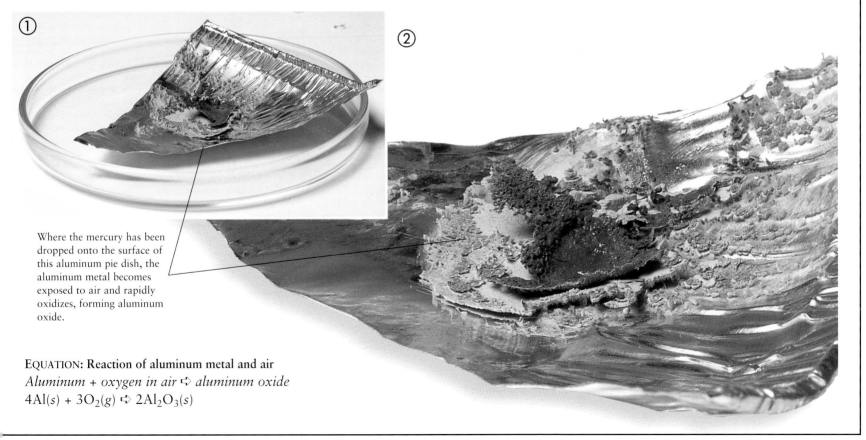

①

②

Where the mercury has been dropped onto the surface of this aluminum pie dish, the aluminum metal becomes exposed to air and rapidly oxidizes, forming aluminum oxide.

EQUATION: Reaction of aluminum metal and air
Aluminum + oxygen in air ⇨ aluminum oxide
$4Al(s) + 3O_2(g) ⇨ 2Al_2O_3(s)$

Metals reacting with water

The most reactive metals (those in Groups 1 and 2 of the Periodic Table) react with water, releasing hydrogen and yielding a metal hydroxide.

The hydroxides produced by Group 1 metals (such as sodium and potassium) are soluble (they are alkalis), while the hydroxides produced by Group 2 metals (such as calcium and barium) are not very soluble (they are, nonetheless, strong bases).

Demonstration 1: sodium and water

If a piece of sodium is dropped into water in a shallow beaker to which phenolphthalein indicator has been added (①), the pellet begins to react immediately. Hydrogen is released in the reaction, propelling the pellet along the surface and forming a fizzing trail (②).

The reaction also produces sodium hydroxide, which is strongly alkaline and makes the phenolphthalein indicator turn pink (② & ③). However, sodium hydroxide is soluble, and so the solution in the beaker remains colorless.

The heat released from the reaction causes the metal to form a rolling molten ball and turns some of the water into steam. The pellet of sodium has completely reacted within 20 seconds.

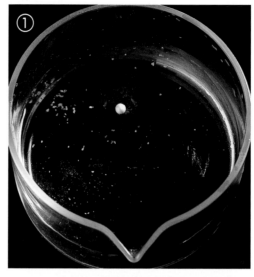

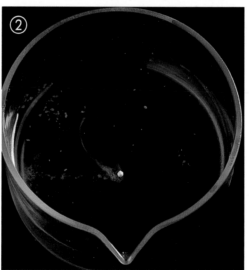

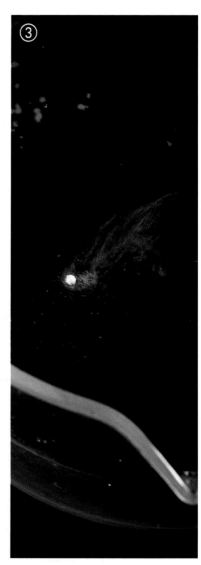

EQUATION: Reaction of sodium metal with water
Sodium + water ⇨ sodium hydroxide + hydrogen
$2Na(s) + 2H_2O(l) ⇨ 2NaOH(aq) + H_2(g)$

14

Demonstration 2: calcium and water

When a small pellet of calcium is placed in a shallow beaker of water, it sinks to the bottom. At this stage an upturned test tube, which has been filled with water, is placed over the pellet.

Calcium forms an oxide coating when exposed to the air. The pellet used in this demonstration had such an oxide layer, which tends to act as a barrier to reaction. It takes a few seconds for the oxide layer to be penetrated, and for the reaction to show any signs of activity.

After this quiet period a reaction begins between the calcium and the water. Hydrogen is released (①) in sufficient quantity for the bubbles to be able to buoy up the calcium pellet and carry it to the surface (②). Here the hydrogen bubbles burst, and the pellet begins to sink until enough new bubbles have formed to raise the pellet to the surface again (③). In this way the calcium pellet bobs up and down in the test tube.

The hydrogen displaces the water from the test tube, and the reaction continues for approximately a minute until all the metal has reacted.

The reaction of the calcium with the water quickly saturates the water in the test tube with calcium hydroxide (also known as limewater). Calcium hydroxide is not very soluble and forms tiny granular particles (PRECIPITATE) that remain suspended in the water, giving the water a cloudy appearance (④).

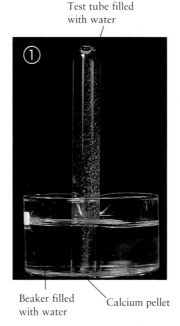

Test tube filled with water

Beaker filled with water

Calcium pellet

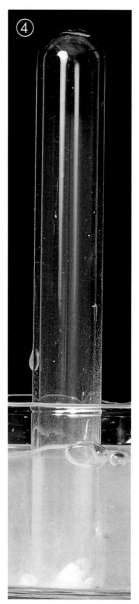

EQUATION: Calcium and water

Calcium + water ⇨ hydrogen gas + calcium hydroxide

$Ca(s) + 2H_2O(l) \Rightarrow H_2(g) + Ca(OH)_2(aq)$

Metals reacting with air and water

Reactions that occur with air and water are different from those that occur with either air or water. The slow changes that occur to metals in the presence of air and water at normal temperatures are called CORROSION. Corrosion normally occurs very quickly, as a transparently thin oxide layer forms on the surface of clean metal. In many cases this oxide layer extends evenly across the metal, wrapping it up in a protective skin of unreactive oxide. However, in certain metals the oxide skin is POROUS, which means that water can still get in. This is the case for iron. The combined presence of water and iron sets up small electrical currents near the surface of the metal, which causes corrosion to work much faster than normal. This effect commonly is called RUSTING.

Demonstration: corrosion of iron

Corrosion of iron requires the presence of both water and air. If an iron nail is placed in a small tube that is partly filled with distilled water and left open to the air (①), the part of the nail in the water will gradually corrode (②). If some similar new clean nails are put in a DESICCATOR (③), a piece of apparatus designed to keep the air completely dry, and if yet more nails are placed in a tube that is then filled with freshly prepared distilled water (which has been boiled in preparation and so contains no dissolved oxygen), little corrosion is seen, even after many weeks, in either case.

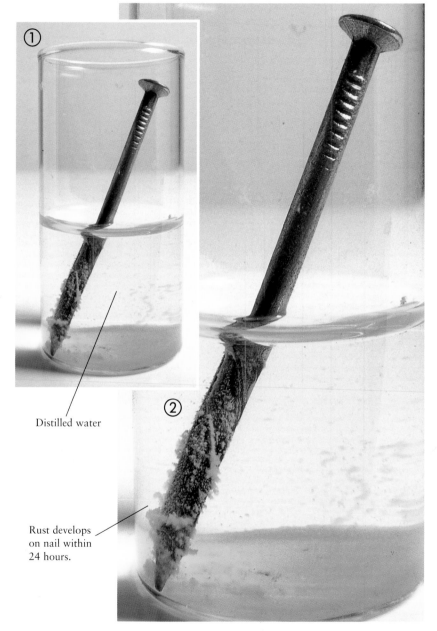

①

Distilled water

②

Rust develops on nail within 24 hours.

The increased corrosion on the nail that is exposed to both water and air is obvious within a few days.

Remarks

Corrosion of iron is an electrochemical effect. The water on the surface is oxygen-rich, and where it meets the iron, it forms an ELECTRODE, one terminal of a battery. The iron in contact with the oxygen-poor region away from the surface water forms the other electrode. The water forms the ELECTROLYTE. A very small electric current now flows, and iron is carried in solution to the oxygen-rich water, where it is OXIDIZED further and deposited.

Thus iron is removed from one part of the metal and deposited as an oxide or hydroxide nearby. This explains why rusty material is often both pitted and lumpy.

③

(Right) This jar is called a desiccator. The blue crystals in the bottom are silica gel colored with cobalt(II) chloride. They absorb any moisture in the air. The nails are therefore in completely dry air. Although they have been sealed in this desiccator for many years, they show no signs of rust. This indicates that both moisture and oxygen are required to form rust.

EQUATION: The rusting of iron
Iron + water + oxygen ⇨ iron(III) hydroxide ⇨ iron(III) oxide + water
$4Fe(s) + 6H_2O(l) + 3O_2(g) \Rightarrow 4Fe(OH)_3(s) \Rightarrow 2Fe_2O_3(s) + 6H_2O(l)$
Rust

Metals reacting with steam

Metals less reactive than potassium and sodium, such as magnesium, require a source of heat energy for a reaction to occur. There is almost no reaction with water or with air at room temperature, and even hot water will not produce a significant reaction. Magnesium has to be heated using a Bunsen flame. Once the reaction has begun, however, it is exothermic, and heat is given out that can maintain the reaction to completion without further heating.

Demonstration: magnesium and steam

In this demonstration a small quantity of mineral (and therefore heat-resistant) wool is soaked in water and placed in the far end of a boiling tube. The tube is clamped horizontally, and a spatula is then used to spread some magnesium granules along the length of the tube.

The end of the tube is fitted with a stopper and a delivery tube, so that the gas coming from the reaction can be collected and tested.

The heating is done with a Bunsen flame. The flame is played evenly along the tube (①), so that the glass heats up slowly, without cracking. Gradually, more and more heat is played on the granules, until they are very hot, and heat then reaches the water at the end of the tube, turning the water into steam. As the steam reaches the granules, a spectacular reaction occurs, the granules burning with an intense white glow (②).

The Bunsen flame is withdrawn from heating the magnesium at this stage, and the white light continues to be emitted as the remaining steam and magnesium react (③). When the reaction is complete, the white material in the tube is an ash of magnesium oxide (④). The gas collected in the gas jar by downward displacement over water is then tested with a flame. A popping sound as the flame is introduced to the gas jar shows the gas to be hydrogen.

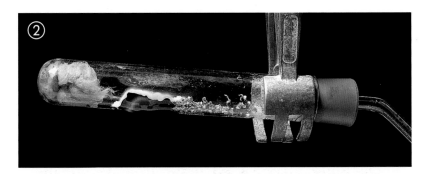

The intense heat produced by this reaction often cracks and then breaks the boiling tube (⑤). The demonstration is thus best done in a fume chamber to prevent accidents with flying glass.

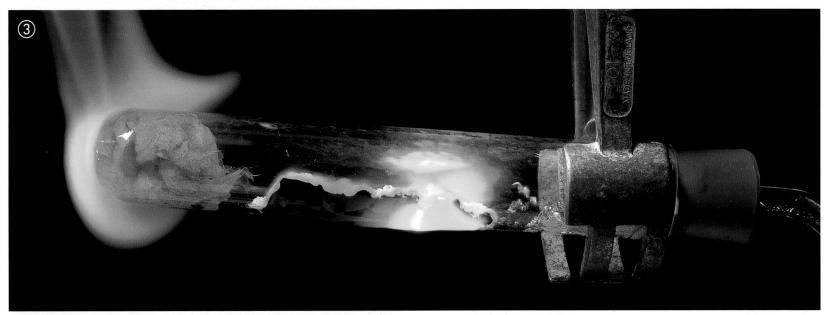

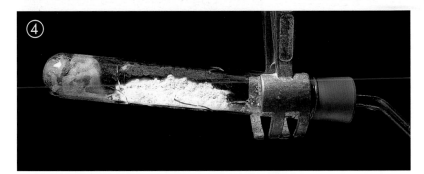

METALS, REACTIVITY, AND SOLUTIONS

The way metals behave in SOLUTIONS is one of the most important aspects of metal chemistry. To understand this, it is necessary to understand that in a solution in which a reaction takes place, the metal atoms lose electrons and become positively charged ions, or cations. (This also means that metals are REDUCING AGENTS.)

You can see this by investigating how a metal reacts with a dilute acid (①, also see page 23 for this demonstration).

EQUATION for the overall reaction

Zinc metal + hydrochloric acid ⇨ zinc chloride + hydrogen
$$Zn(s) + 2HCl(aq) ⇨ ZnCl_2(aq) + H_2(g)$$

①
Dilute hydrochloric acid is added.

Pieces of zinc metal

Hydrogen gas can be seen as bubbles.

Solution of zinc chloride

But two stages have actually occurred:

(STAGE 1) The part of the zinc that has reacted with the acid has lost electrons to become $Zn^{2+}(aq)$ (positive cations in solution).

IONIC EQUATION: Zinc metal to zinc ions

Zinc metal + hydrogen ions in acid ⇨ zinc ions + hydrogen gas
$$Zn(s) + 2H^+(aq) ⇨ Zn^{2+}(aq) + H_2(g)$$

(STAGE 2) The acid has broken up (become ionized) into ions.

Hydrochloric acid ⇨ H^+ and Cl^- ions
$$HCl(aq) ⇨ H^+(aq) + Cl^-(aq)$$

The chloride ions are spectator ions (i.e., they are unchanged).

Chloride ions in hydrochloric acid ⇨ chloride ions in zinc chloride
$$Cl^-(aq) ⇨ Cl^-(aq)$$

The hydrogen ions accept the electrons released from the zinc, allowing the hydrogen ions to form hydrogen molecules and come out of solution as a gas.

Hydrogen ions + electrons ⇨ hydrogen molecules
$$2H^+(aq) + 2e^- ⇨ H_2(g)$$

This leaves the zinc and the chloride ions to come together to form the new product, zinc chloride. (If the solution is concentrated by evaporation, a colorless, crystalline solid forms.) In this case, because zinc chloride is soluble, it stays in solution as a colorless SOLUTE.

$$Zn^{2+}(aq) + 2Cl^-(aq) \Rightarrow ZnCl_2(aq)$$

So, every chemical reaction of this kind involves two "half reactions" of charged particles.

Reactivity of metals

Some metals will react more readily than others. For example, when copper is placed in dilute hydrochloric acid, no reaction appears to occur at all. Thus not all metals are equally reactive. The relative reactivities of metals commonly available in the laboratory can be seen from the table to the right (②). If this is compared with the Periodic Table, it is noticeable that the most reactive metals are at the left-hand side of the table (and in Groups 1 and 2). In practice the true reactivity of many other metals may be obscured by a protective layer of oxide. This is particularly true for aluminum.

(Left) Calcium is in Group 2 of the Periodic Table and so is a relatively reactive metal. When exposed to air, the silvery metal is readily oxidized and forms a dull oxide coating, as can be seen with these pellets. This protective layer must be penetrated before a reaction can take place with the pure metal.

②	THE METAL REACTIVITY SERIES			
Element	**Metallic form** *(reduced form)*	**Ionic form** *(oxidized form)*	**Reactivity**	**Reducing power**
Potassium	K	K$^+$		*most strongly reducing*
Sodium	Na	Na$^+$		
Calcium	Ca	Ca^{2+}		
Magnesium	Mg	Mg^{2+}		
Aluminum	Al	Al^{3+}		
Manganese	Mn	Mn^{2+}		
Chromium	Cr	Cr^{2+}		
Zinc	Zn	Zn^{2+}		
Iron	Fe	Fe^{2+}	*increasing reactivity*	
Cadmium	Cd	Cd^{2+}		
Tin	Sn	Sn^{2+}		
Lead	Pb	Pb^{2+}		
Hydrogen	H$_2$	H$^+$		
Copper	Cu	Cu^{2+}		
Mercury	Hg	Hg^{2+}		
Silver	Ag	Ag$^+$		
Gold	Au	Au$^+$		*least strongly reducing*
Platinum	Pt	Pt$^+$		

Reactions of reactive metals and acids

All ACIDS contain hydrogen. If a metal is more reactive than hydrogen (and so is higher up the reactivity series than hydrogen (①)), the reaction of the metal with the acid will yield hydrogen gas. This is because the metal atoms will replace (displace) the hydrogen atoms of acids (directly or indirectly), allowing hydrogen atoms to pair up to be hydrogen molecules and be released as hydrogen gas. The remaining solution will be a metal salt.

Thus, for example, magnesium, zinc, iron, and tin react with sulfuric or hydrochloric acid to produce hydrogen gas and the corresponding salt (such as magnesium chloride in the case of hydrochloric acid and magnesium).

Demonstration 1: reaction of magnesium and hydrochloric acid

When a piece of magnesium ribbon (that has been scraped clean to remove the oxide layer) is dropped into a beaker containing dilute hydrochloric acid (②), a reaction takes place in which hydrogen gas is given off. The reaction is exothermic, so the beaker becomes warm, and steam is evolved together with the gas. This is seen as steamy fumes (③). The salt is (colorless) soluble magnesium chloride.

① REACTIVITY SERIES

Element	Reactivity
potassium	most reactive
sodium	
calcium	
magnesium	
aluminum	
manganese	
chromium	
zinc	
iron	
cadmium	
tin	
lead	
hydrogen	
copper	
mercury	
silver	
gold	
platinum	least reactive

EQUATION: Magnesium and hydrochloric acid

Magnesium + dilute hydrochloric acid ⇨ magnesium chloride + hydrogen

$Mg(s) + 2HCl(aq) ⇨ MgCl_2(aq) + H_2(g)$

Demonstration 2: reaction of zinc and sulfuric acid

When dilute sulfuric acid is poured over a piece of sheet zinc (④), a reaction takes place in which hydrogen gas is given off. Zinc (which is below magnesium in the reactivity series) is less reactive than magnesium, and so the reaction proceeds less vigorously than in demonstration 1 (⑤). Thus, although considerable bubbling occurs, the reaction is less exothermic, and steam is not evolved (⑥). The salt produced in this case is soluble zinc sulfate, which forms as a colorless solution.

EQUATION: Zinc and sulfuric acid

Zinc + sulfuric acid ⇨ zinc sulfate + hydrogen

$Zn(s) + H_2SO_4(aq) ⇨ ZnSO_4(s) + H_2(g)$

Reactions of less reactive metals and acids

Copper and other metals below it in the reactivity series do not displace hydrogen directly from acids and so do not produce hydrogen gas (①). These metals will only react with acids that are also very strong OXIDIZING AGENTS, such as nitric acid and concentrated sulfuric acid.

Demonstration 1: reaction of mercury and nitric acid

When fuming nitric acid is poured onto liquid mercury in a beaker (②), strong effervescence occurs, and brown fumes are given off (③). The product left in the beaker is mercury(II) nitrate; the gas given off is brown nitrogen dioxide. The heat of the exothermic reaction also boils off some of the water, which accounts for the steamy nature of the fumes.

① **REACTIVITY SERIES**

Element	Reactivity
potassium	most reactive
sodium	
calcium	
magnesium	
aluminium	
manganese	
chromium	
zinc	
iron	
cadmium	
tin	
lead	
hydrogen	
copper	
mercury	
silver	
gold	
platinum	least reactive

Concentrated nitric acid is poured onto mercury.

Brown nitrogen dioxide gas

EQUATION: Reaction of mercury and nitric acid

Mercury + concentrated nitric acid ⇨ mercury(II) nitrate + water + nitrogen dioxide

$Hg(s) + 4HNO_3(conc) \Rightarrow Hg(NO_3)_2(aq) + 2H_2O(l) + 2NO_2(g)$

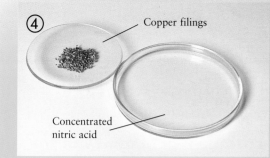
④ Copper filings

Concentrated nitric acid

Demonstration 2: reaction of copper and nitric acid

When nitric acid is poured into a Petri dish containing orange-colored copper filings (④), strong effervescence occurs, and a green coloration appears (⑤). A brown gas is evolved (⑥ & ⑦). The product left in the dish is (blue) copper(II) nitrate, the gas evolved is brown nitrogen dioxide gas, and the heat of the exothermic reaction causes water to boil off as steam, accounting for the steamy nature of the fumes.

Remarks

Mercury is a poisonous liquid, mercury vapor and nitrogen dioxide are poisonous gases, and fuming nitric acid is a powerful oxidizing agent that can harm skin. These demonstrations are therefore performed in a fume chamber using appropriate protective equipment.

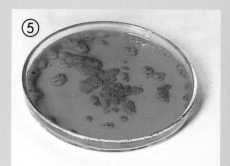
⑤

⑥

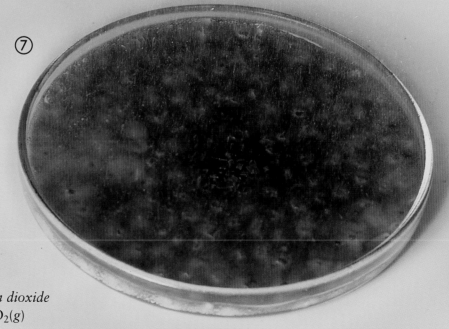
⑦

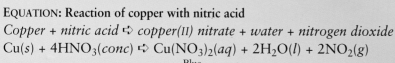
EQUATION: Reaction of copper with nitric acid

Copper + nitric acid ⇨ copper(II) nitrate + water + nitrogen dioxide

$Cu(s) + 4HNO_3(conc) \Rightarrow Cu(NO_3)_2(aq) + 2H_2O(l) + 2NO_2(g)$
Blue

Metals that react with acids and alkalis

①

A metal that will react with alkalis as well as with acids is called an AMPHOTERIC metal. The most common metals with this property are aluminum, zinc, and lead. These are all nearer the center of the Periodic Table than the most reactive metals in Group 1.

Demonstration 1: reaction of aluminum and sodium hydroxide

Sodium hydroxide is a strong ALKALI. When a piece of aluminum foil is placed in a Petri dish (①) and some warm concentrated sodium hydroxide is dropped onto it from a pipette, a reaction takes place immediately, and steam is produced (②).

The reaction is fierce enough to cause the aluminum to rise and fall with the bubbles of hydrogen formed by the reaction on the underside of the aluminum.

Within two minutes the aluminum has been removed completely from the central region where the sodium hydroxide has been applied (③).

Warm concentrated sodium hydroxide is dripped onto the aluminum foil.

②

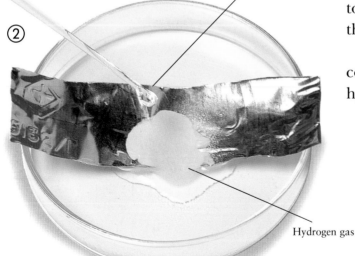

Hydrogen gas

③

EQUATION: Aluminum and sodium hydroxide
Aluminum + concentrated sodium hydroxide + water ⇨ sodium aluminate + hydrogen
$2Al(s) + 2NaOH(conc) + 6H_2O(l) \Rightarrow 2NaAl(OH)_4(aq) + 3H_2(g)$

Demonstration 2: reaction of zinc and sodium hydroxide

When warm, concentrated sodium hydroxide is dropped onto zinc sheet in a comparable test to the aluminum (page 26), the reaction is far more subdued (④). However, when a catalyst is added in the form of Devarda's alloy (zinc with added copper), the reaction is more rapid. If coarse powdered zinc is used (to make a greater surface area for reaction), instant evolution of hydrogen is observed (⑤ & ⑥).

Remarks

When a metal is amphoteric, the oxide and the hydroxide of the metal are also amphoteric and may produce a reaction that is easier to see. For example, a zinc compound will react with sodium hydroxide to produce a precipitate of insoluble zinc hydroxide; then the hydroxide "redissolves" in excess alkali, a demonstration that can be done in a test tube.

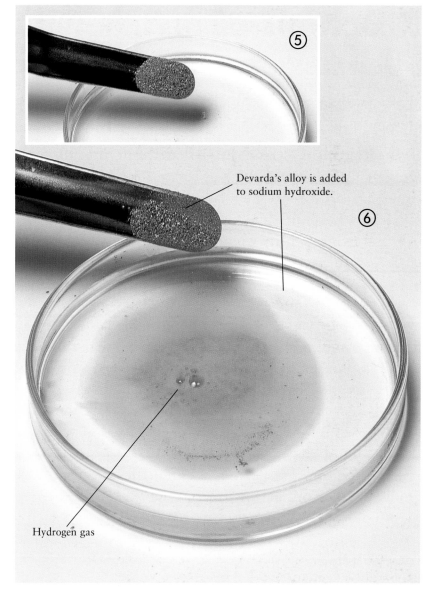

⑤

⑥

Devarda's alloy is added to sodium hydroxide.

Hydrogen gas

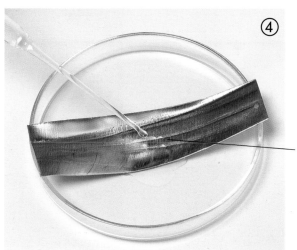

④

Warm, concentrated, sodium hydroxide is dripped onto the zinc sheet.

EQUATION: Zinc (Devarda's alloy) and sodium hydroxide

Zinc + concentrated sodium hydroxide + water ⇨ sodium zincate + hydrogen

$2Zn(s) + 2NaOH(conc) + 6H_2O(l) \Rightarrow 2NaZn(OH)_4(aq) + 3H_2(g)$

Copper catalyst

Reactions of metals with the halogens

Metals can act as reducing agents. They will therefore react with oxidizing agents such as the HALOGENS to produce a salt. The halogens are the nonmetal elements in Group 7 of the Periodic Table.

Demonstration 1: reaction of sodium and chlorine

All the Group 1 metals, such as sodium and potassium, react with chlorine gas to produce a salt.

To demonstrate this, a gas jar of chlorine gas is first prepared by reacting dilute hydrochloric acid with potassium permanganate (①). Chlorine is more dense than air and soluble in water, and so the gas is collected by upward displacement of air.

A small pellet of sodium is placed in a combustion "spoon" made from a ceramic crucible or a crucible lid. If the spoon was made of iron, the iron would also combust! (②) It is heated in the air with a Bunsen flame until it begins to burn. The burning sodium is now lowered into the gas jar containing the chlorine. Because chlorine is a very reactive oxidizing gas, the sodium continues to burn (the chlorine is being used to aid combustion) (③). As the sodium burns, a white smoke is formed. This is a precipitate of tiny particles of sodium chloride, a halide salt, which gradually settle out on the walls and bottom of the gas jar and in the bowl of the combustion spoon (④ & ⑤).

EQUATION: Preparation of chlorine
Concentrated hydrochloric acid + potassium permanganate ⇨ chlorine + water + manganese(II) chloride + potassium chloride
$16HCl(aq) + 2KMnO_4(s) ⇨ 5Cl_2(g) + 8H_2O(l) + 2MnCl_2(aq) + 2KCl(aq)$

EQUATION: Reaction of sodium and chlorine
Sodium + chlorine ⇨ sodium chloride
$2Na(s) + Cl_2(g) ⇨ 2NaCl(s)$

①

NOTE: Because halogen gases are poisonous, the demonstrations are conducted in a fume chamber.

②

Sodium pellet is placed in crucible lid.

Gas jar of chlorine gas

③ ④ ⑤

White deposit of sodium chloride

Demonstration 2: reaction of iron and chlorine

Chlorine will react with iron (in the form of steel wool) that is strongly heated to produce red light and produce a large amount of reddish smoke.

The apparatus consists of a system for generating chlorine, a combustion tube in which the steel wool is heated, and a collecting vessel, in this case a side-arm conical flask connected to a suction pump that will allow the chlorine to pass through the apparatus and also remove any unreacted chlorine at the end of the reaction (⑥). Since chlorine gas is poisonous, all of the apparatus is placed in a fume chamber during the demonstration.

Chlorine gas is first generated by reacting concentrated hydrochloric acid from a dropper funnel with potassium permanganate in a conical flask and then fed into a combustion tube (made of a heat-resistant glass) containing steel wool.

The steel wool is heated strongly (⑦), and eventually it begins to flare up into yellow and red colors, the flaring section slowly making its way along the tube as the iron is consumed (⑧).

The Bunsen flame can be taken away at this stage because the reaction is exothermic, and enough internal heat is generated to continue the reaction unaided (⑨ & ⑩).

Reddish smoke containing tiny iron(III) chloride particles begins to form and flows out to the collecting flask, gradually precipitating on the bottom of the flask (⑪, page 32).

EQUATION: Reaction of iron and chlorine
Iron + chlorine ➪ iron(III) chloride
$$2Fe(s) + 3Cl_2(g) \rightarrow 2FeCl_3(s)$$

The dropper funnel allows for a controlled release of hydrochloric acid onto the potassium permanganate to generate chlorine.

A suction pump draws off waste fumes from a side-arm flask.

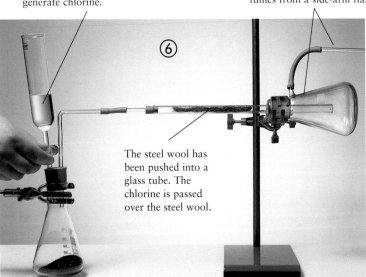

⑥

The steel wool has been pushed into a glass tube. The chlorine is passed over the steel wool.

⑦

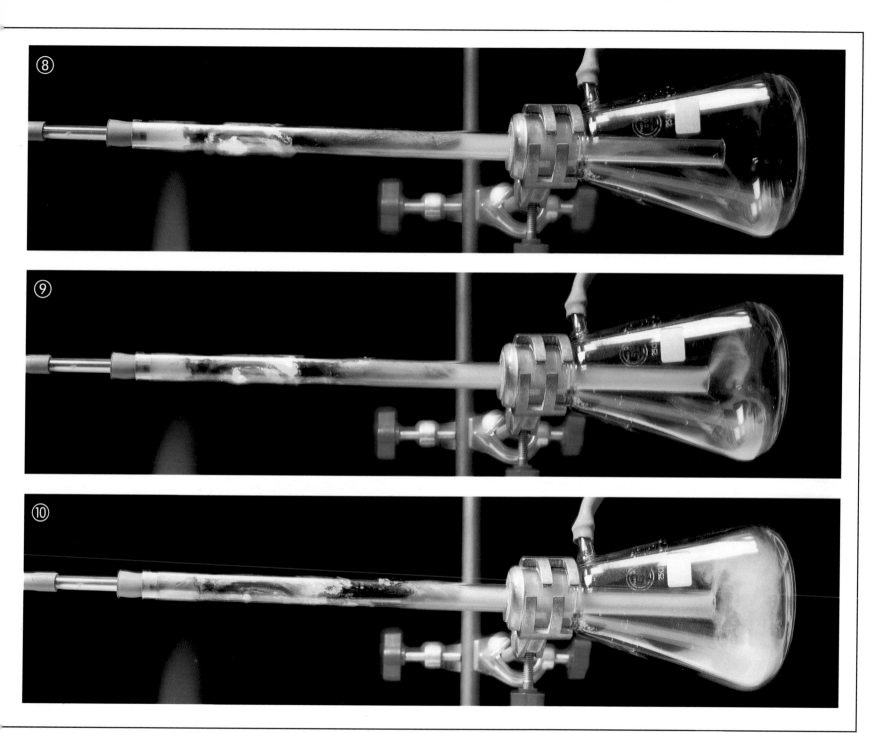

⑪

Demonstration 3: reaction of aluminum and chlorine

Chlorine will react violently and spectacularly with aluminum that is heated strongly, producing an intense white light.

The apparatus consists of a system for generating chlorine, a combustion tube in which the aluminum is heated, and a collecting vessel, in this case a side-arm conical flask connected to a suction pump that will allow the chlorine to flow through the apparatus and also remove any unreacted chlorine at the end of the reaction (⑫). Since chlorine gas is poisonous, all of the apparatus is placed in a fume chamber during the demonstration.

Chlorine gas is first generated by reacting concentrated hydrochloric acid from a dropper funnel with potassium permanganate in the conical flask and is then fed into a combustion tube (made of a heat-resistant glass) containing aluminum foil.

The aluminum foil is heated strongly (⑬), and

eventually it begins to flare (⑭). An intense white light emanates from the burning aluminum (⑮, page 34), while a pale yellow smoke consisting of fine particles of aluminum chloride flows into the flask (⑯). The Bunsen flame can be taken away at this stage because the reaction is exothermic, and enough internal heat is generated to continue the reaction unaided. A pale yellow crust of aluminum chloride is left as a deposit inside the tube (⑰, page 35) and the side-arm flask (⑱).

The aluminum foil has been pushed into a glass tube. The chlorine is passed over the aluminum foil.

⑫

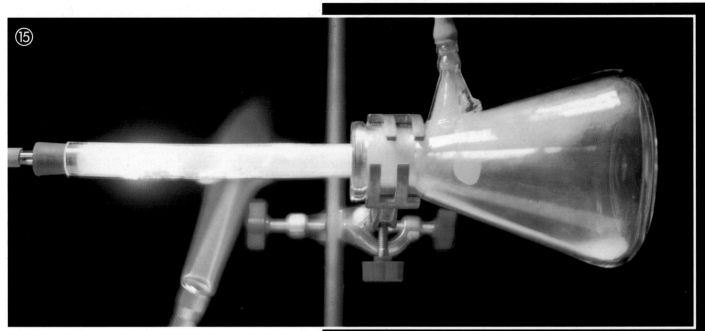

EQUATION: Reaction of aluminum and chlorine
Aluminum + chlorine ⇨ aluminum(III) chloride
$2Al(s) + 3Cl_2(g) ⇨ 2AlCl_3(s)$

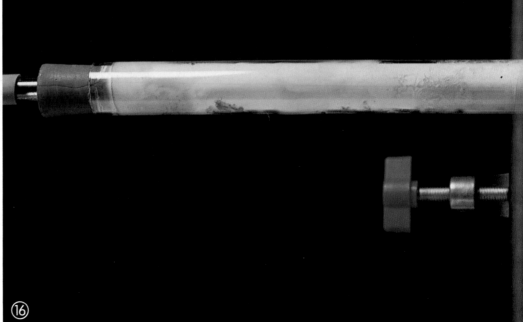

Yellow deposit of
aluminum chloride

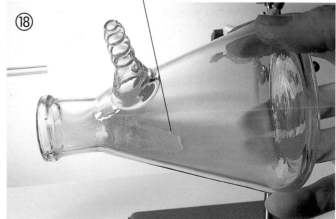

Demonstration 4: reaction of iron and bromine

A small amount of bromine is poured into the bottom of a boiling tube. Some steel wool is fed into the tube so that it is about halfway along (⑲). The steel wool is then heated strongly, causing the bromine to vaporize.

The reaction between bromine and iron is exothermic once started. The steel wool begins to flare. Brownish fumes of iron(III) bromide form and flow along the tube, where they condense as they cool to form brown crystals (⑳).

Demonstration 5: reaction of aluminum and iodine

Aluminum powder is added to a small pile of iodine crystals on a heat-resistant gauze disk, and the powder and crystals mixed together (㉑). In this dry state nothing happens. However, when distilled water is dropped onto the mixture (㉒), a reaction occurs that produces dense purple iodine fumes (㉓). Once the reaction is complete, a deposit containing aluminum iodide is left on the gauze (㉔).

Remarks

In this case the water acts as a catalyst. The reaction can also be started by friction between the reactants. To avoid this problem, mixing is done gently and with care.

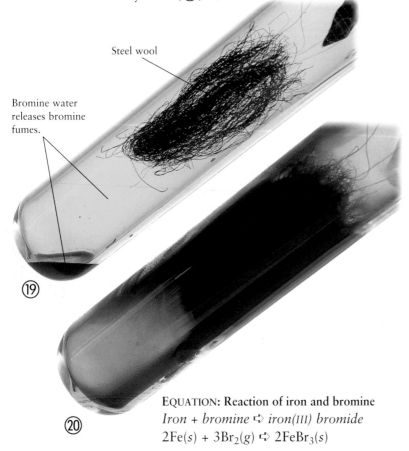

Steel wool

Bromine water releases bromine fumes.

⑲

⑳

EQUATION: Reaction of iron and bromine
Iron + bromine ➪ iron(III) bromide
$2Fe(s) + 3Br_2(g) ➪ 2FeBr_3(s)$

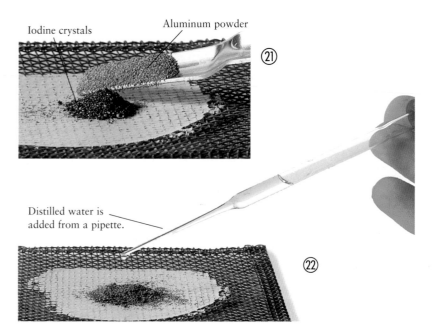

Iodine crystals

Aluminum powder

㉑

Distilled water is added from a pipette.

㉒

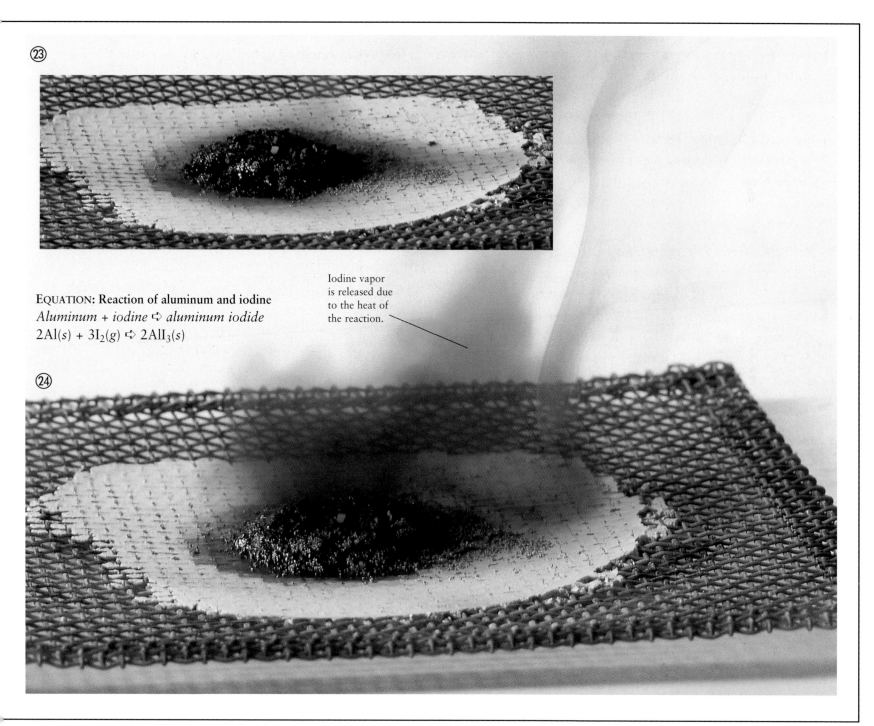

㉓

EQUATION: Reaction of aluminum and iodine
Aluminum + iodine ⇨ aluminum iodide
$2Al(s) + 3I_2(g) ⇨ 2AlI_3(s)$

Iodine vapor is released due to the heat of the reaction.

㉔

Measuring reaction rates of magnesium and zinc

This is an example of a quantitative demonstration. Instead of just watching a demonstration to see what happens, the purpose here is to find the quantities involved in the reaction. To achieve this, each of the reactants must be accurately measured. The reactants are weighed to find their masses, and the volume of the gas evolved over time is recorded.

Demonstration 1: measuring the gas evolved on reaction

This demonstration will compare the reaction rates of two metals, magnesium and zinc. It uses a conical flask containing a known volume of acid of known concentration and a small tube containing a known weight (mass) of metal.

The acid (in this case hydrochloric acid) is placed in the conical flask. Because it is important to measure the gas evolved, all precautions must be taken to prevent the escape of the gas, so the stopper and delivery tube must be almost in place before the reaction starts. To achieve this, a small test tube containing the known mass of metal powder is suspended by a thread (①) and released into the conical flask as the stopwatch is started, and the stopper is then immediately tightened down (②). By using the stopwatch and a graduated tube, the time taken to produce 50 cm^3 of gas can be measured.

For this to be a fair test between the reactivity of magnesium and zinc, it is necessary to use:
(a) the same volume of the same concentration of hydrochloric acid solution at the same temperature,
(b) the same amount of metal each time.

This latter requirement cannot be satisfied simply by using the same MASS of metal, since the atoms have different masses. The same number of atoms is contained in 0.65 g of zinc (③) and 0.24 g of magnesium (④). However, as can be seen if these masses of the powders are compared, the surface area of the zinc (⑤) is much less than that of the magnesium (⑥). Since the acid reacts with the surface of the metal, to make the reactions comparable, the amount of metal surface should be the same in both demonstrations. The third tube (⑦) shows zinc powder of comparable volume to the magnesium. The mass of this was found to be 1.49 g (⑧).

Remarks

The time taken to produce 50 cm^3 of gas when magnesium was the reactant (test tube ⑥) was 6.4 seconds (⑨ & ⑩, page 40). When the same number of atoms of zinc was used (test tube ⑤), the time to yield 50 cm^3 of gas was 300 seconds (⑪, page 40).

Even when the same volume (surface area) of zinc was used (test tube ⑦), it took 280 seconds to yield 50 cm^3 of gas, showing that the magnesium is much more reactive with an acid than zinc is.

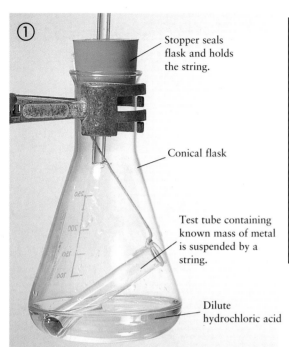

① Stopper seals flask and holds the string.

Conical flask

Test tube containing known mass of metal is suspended by a string.

Dilute hydrochloric acid

(Below) The container is placed on the scale, and the balance is reset to zero (TARED).

0.00g

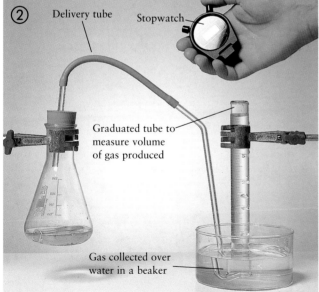

② Delivery tube

Stopwatch

Graduated tube to measure volume of gas produced

Gas collected over water in a beaker

③ 0.65g

⑤

⑥

⑦

0.65 g zinc powder

0.24 g magnesium powder

1.49 g zinc powder

④ 0.24g

⑧ 1.49g

Demonstration 2: measuring the heat evolved on reaction

Another measure of the reactivity of a reaction is the heat evolved. This can be done in a number of ways, but all involve measuring the temperature rise of the solution during the reaction.

As this is a quantitative demonstration, the amount of each reactant used must be the same in each reaction so that a fair comparative test is achieved.

A simple apparatus that can measure the rise in temperature during a reaction is a CALORIMETER. This is named after the former unit for heat, the calorie.

The purpose of a calorimeter is to prevent loss of heat to the surroundings. Thus the calorimeter is essentially an insulating container. For most purposes a calorimeter can be made up using glass beakers and polystyrene foam disposable cups because the cups and the air gaps between them have very good insulating properties.

As in the demonstration on page 38, a known volume of dilute hydrochloric acid is reacted with a known mass of reactant (in this case, powdered magnesium or zinc). The acid is first placed in the polystyrene cup, and its temperature taken with a stirring thermometer (⑫).

The metal is then added (⑬), and the solution stirred, noting all the time the rise in temperature that results from the reaction. When the highest temperature has been reached, this is recorded. The difference between the highest temperature and the starting temperature is then a measure of the reactivity of the metal.

In this demonstration the reaction of magnesium and dilute hydrochloric acid produced a maximum temperature difference of 25°C, while the zinc reaction produced a maximum temperature difference of 11°C, showing the magnesium is more reactive than zinc.

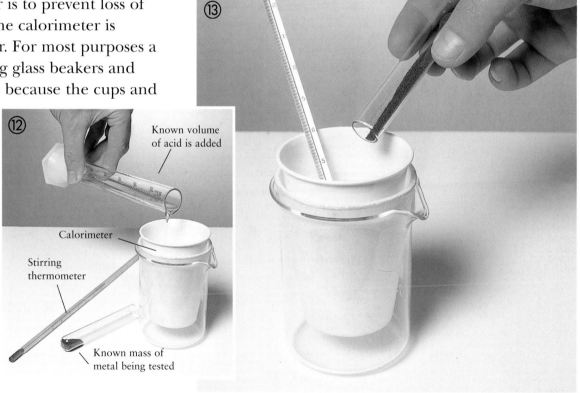

⑫ Known volume of acid is added

Calorimeter

Stirring thermometer

Known mass of metal being tested

⑬

Displacement reactions between metals

Because metals differ in their reactivity, if a more reactive metal is placed in a solution of a less reactive metal compound, a reaction occurs in which the more reactive metal displaces the metal ions in the solution. For example, when zinc metal is introduced into a solution of copper(II) sulfate (which thus contains copper ions), zinc goes into solution as zinc ions, while copper is displaced from the solution and forced to precipitate as metallic copper.

EQUATION TO SHOW IONS

Zinc metal + copper ions ⇨ *zinc ions + copper metal*

$Zn(s) + Cu^{2+}(aq) ⇨ Zn^{2+}(aq) + Cu(s)$

In this reaction zinc atoms lose two electrons (and dissolve), and the copper ions each gain those two electrons, becoming metal atoms.

Remarks

These displacement reactions take place spontaneously; and because the reaction involves the movement of electrons, it has generated an electric current. All of the following demonstrations therefore show reactions that are similar to the reactions in a battery.

To speed up the displacement process, it helps to move the metal around in the solution or to stir the solution with a glass rod. In this way the ions in the solution are brought to the metal surface more rapidly than they would have been by DIFFUSION.

Creating a displacement matrix

It is possible to investigate the relative reducing abilities of the metals by conducting a series of demonstrations using a metal strip placed in a solution containing a salt of a different metal, as shown here.

DISPLACEMENT REACTION TABLE						
Metal ions / **Metals**	Mg^{2+}	Zn^{2+}	Fe^{2+}	Pb^{2+}	Cu^{2+}	Ag^+
Magnesium (Mg)	✘	✔	✔	✔	✔	✔
Zinc (Zn)	✘	✘	✔	✔	✔	✔
Iron (Fe)	✘	✘	✘	✔	✔	✔
Lead (Pb)	✘	✘	✘	✘	✔	✔
Copper (Cu)	✘	✘	✘	✘	✘	✔
Silver (Ag)	✘	✘	✘	✘	✘	✘

(Decreasing reactivity ↓)

The displacement reaction table

The table to the left shows metals in order of decreasing reactivity.

A metal will displace any less reactive metal from a solution containing ions of the less reactive metal (i.e., an appropriate salt solution).

✔ = displacement takes place

✘ = reaction does not take place

● = demonstrated on the next four pages

Demonstration 1: magnesium displacing iron

A magnesium strip is placed in a bottle containing an almost colorless solution of iron(II) sulfate.

Result: The magnesium strip changes extremely rapidly.

EQUATION TO SHOW IONS
$$Mg(s) + Fe^{2+}(aq) \rightarrow Mg^{2+}(aq) + Fe(s)$$

The magnesium metal displaces the iron from the iron(II) sulfate, precipitating iron on the magnesium strip, and some hydrogen gas is evolved (①). The turbulence resulting from the evolution of hydrogen dislodges the small particles of iron precipitated around the magnesium ribbon, and they fall away (②).

Demonstration 2: magnesium displacing lead

A magnesium strip is placed in a bottle containing a colorless solution of lead nitrate (③).

Result: The magnesium strip changes very rapidly.

EQUATION TO SHOW IONS
$$Mg(s) + Pb^{2+}(aq) \rightarrow Mg^{2+}(aq) + Pb(s)$$

The magnesium metal displaces the lead from the lead nitrate, precipitating lead on the magnesium strip (④). The particle size increases to a point where reflection from the surface of the lead crystals is apparent as a shiny sheen.

Demonstration 3: magnesium displacing silver

A magnesium strip is placed in a bottle containing a colorless solution of silver nitrate (⑤).

Result: The magnesium strip changes rapidly.

EQUATION TO SHOW IONS

$$Mg(s) + 2Ag^+(aq) \Rightarrow Mg^{2+}(aq) + 2Ag(s)$$

The magnesium metal displaces the silver from the silver nitrate, precipitating silver on the magnesium strip (⑥). At first the small particles look black, but within a few minutes they build up enough to show a characteristic silver-colored metallic luster.

Demonstration 4: zinc displacing silver

A zinc strip is placed in a Petri dish containing silver nitrate (⑦).

Result: The zinc strip changes quite rapidly.

EQUATION TO SHOW ION MOVEMENTS

$$Zn(s) + Ag^+(aq) \Rightarrow Zn^{2+}(aq) + 2Ag(s)$$

The zinc metal displaces the silver from the silver nitrate, precipitating silver on the zinc strip (⑧). At first, the small particles look black, but within a few minutes they build up enough to show a characteristic silver-colored metallic luster.

Demonstration 5: iron displacing copper

An iron nail is placed in a Petri dish containing copper(II) sulfate solution (⑨).

Result: The iron nail changes rapidly.

EQUATION TO SHOW IONS

$Fe(s) + Cu^{2+}(aq) \rightarrow Fe^{2+}(aq) + Cu(s)$

The iron metal displaces the copper from the copper(II) sulfate, precipitating copper on the iron nail (⑩). Within a few minutes a red-pink copper coating becomes visible on the nail (⑪ & ⑫).

Demonstration 6: iron displacing silver

An iron nail is placed in a bottle containing a solution of silver nitrate (⑬).

Result: The iron nail changes slowly.

EQUATION TO SHOW IONS

$Fe(s) + 2Ag^+(aq) \rightarrow Fe^{2+}(aq) + 2Ag(s)$

The iron metal displaces the silver from the silver nitrate, precipitating silver on the iron nail. Silver is precipitated in a shiny layer, plating the surface of the iron nail (⑭). This effectively stops further reaction.

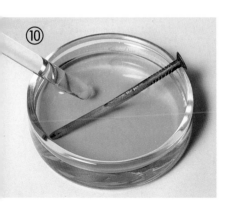

Demonstration 7: copper displacing silver

A copper strip is placed in a bottle containing a solution of silver nitrate.
Result: The copper strip changes slowly.

EQUATION TO SHOW IONS
$$Cu(s) + 2Ag^+(aq) \Rightarrow Cu^{2+}(aq) + 2Ag(s)$$

The copper metal displaces the silver from the silver nitrate, precipitating silver on the copper strip (⑮). The particle size increases to a point where reflection from the surface of the silver crystals is apparent as a metallic luster (⑯).

As the concentration of the copper ions in the solution increases, the solution appears distinctly blue (⑰).

Demonstration 8: copper will not displace zinc

A copper strip is placed in a bottle containing a solution of zinc sulfate (⑱).
Result: The copper strip does not change, so no displacement reaction takes place.

Metal-metal displacement reactions

The reactivity of metals relative to one another can be demonstrated by placing two metals in contact in an electroyte. The liquids in both bottles contain an indicator that turns purple when a reaction takes place.

Demonstration 1: reaction of iron and magnesium

An iron nail with a small piece of magnesium ribbon wrapped around it is placed in a small bottle of water (①).

Within a few minutes a reaction takes place at the magnesium strip, causing the formation of magnesium hydroxide, an alkaline substance that makes the indicator turn purple. The iron nail is not corroded because magnesium is more reactive than iron.

Demonstration 2: reaction of iron and tin

An iron nail with a small piece of tin strip wrapped around it is placed in another bottle of water (②).

Within a few minutes the iron nail has corroded (rusted). This is because iron is more reactive than tin.

Iron nail

Tin strip

Rust

(Above left) **The principle illustrated by this chemistry demonstration is called cathodic protection. It is used widely to protect structures that are made out of iron and are prone to corrosion by rusting, such as the steel hulls of ships, pipelines, oil or gas storage tanks, and bridges. A piece or layer (in the case of galvanizing) of a metal that is higher up the reactivity series than iron is attached to the iron structure. It will corrode first, thus saving the structure. The metal used in cathodic protection is frequently zinc because it is relatively cheap, but occasionally magnesium is used. When applied in this way, these metals are said to be sacrificial anodes.**

Metals as catalysts

A catalyst is a substance that can speed up the rate of a chemical reaction and yet remain unchanged at the end of the reaction.

Catalysts tend to be very specific, so a catalyst that works successfully with one reaction may not work at all in a reaction involving different reactants. However, when catalysts do work, they can increase the rate of a chemical reaction spectacularly, as this demonstration shows.

Demonstration: a metal as a catalyst

Colorless hydrogen peroxide solution is added to colorless sodium potassium tartrate solution, and a relatively slow reaction occurs (①). There is a slow evolution of gas, showing that the reaction is proceeding. Stirring the solution makes the evolution of gas more obvious because the two solutions will be mixed more thoroughly, and the reagents brought more efficiently into contact.

Cobalt(II) chloride solution is added to the mixture (②). The cobalt chloride is added to the top of the mixture, so that the contrast between the original reaction rate and the rate enhanced by the catalyst can be seen

Bubbles of oxygen gas

⑤ ⑥ ⑦

clearly. The cobalt chloride is pink initially, but it darkens over the next few minutes and then changes color. More bubbles can be seen in the dark part of the mixture than in the colorless mixture below (③ & ④).

Within a few seconds the pink color changes to green (⑤) as the catalyst begins to take more effect, and vigorous frothing begins. Notice that because the mixture including the cobalt(II) chloride is less dense than the mixture without it, almost no mixing takes place in the region below, and this region remains colorless.

To demonstrate that the catalyst has not been used up during this reaction, the whole gas jar is now stirred so that the slowly reacting mixture in the bottom of the gas jar is brought into contact with the cobalt chloride.

Vigorous foaming occurs immediately throughout the liquid (⑥). Within two minutes the reaction is complete, and the mixture turns pink again (⑦). At the same time, the effervescence stops.

The solution returns to pink because the catalyst is regenerated (catalysts are unchanged at the end of a reaction).

EQUATION: Catalytic decomposition of hydrogen peroxide using cobalt(II) chloride
Hydrogen peroxide ⇨ water + oxygen
$H_2O_2(aq) ⇨ H_2O(l) + O_2(g)$
Catalyst of cobalt(II) chloride ($CoCl_2$)

EXTRACTING AND REFINING METALS IN THE LABORATORY

There is a close relationship between the position of a metal in the reactivity series and the stability of its compounds. The higher a metal is in the reactivity series, the more stable are its compounds, and the more energy is needed to break them down. Where a metal is amphoteric and reacts with both an acid and an alkali, then so do some of its compounds. However, apart from these similarities, the properties of metals and their compounds are usually different.

Extracting metals from their ores

The reactivity series helps to provide a framework to explain why metals are extracted from their ORES in various ways. Metals high in the reactivity series, for example, are very reactive, and their compounds (ores) are not split apart easily. As a result, very large amounts of energy are required in the form of electrical energy. ELECTROLYSIS is used to obtain aluminum, magnesium, calcium, sodium, and

SOME IMPORTANT METALS AND THEIR PRINCIPAL ORES			
Metals	**Common ore**	**Chief chemical constituent of ore**	**Chemical formula of chief constituent**
Sodium	Rock salt	Sodium chloride	NaCl
Potassium	Seawater	Potassium chloride	KCl
Calcium	Limestone	Calcium carbonate	$CaCO_3$
Magnesium	Carnallite Dolomite	Potassium magnesium chloride Magnesium calcium carbonate	$MgCl_2 \bullet KCl \bullet 6H_2O$ $MgCO_3 \bullet CaCO_3$
Iron	Hematite	Iron(III) oxide	Fe_2O_3
Copper	Copper pyrites	Copper(II) iron(II) sulfide	CuFeS
Zinc	Sphalerite Smithsonite	Zinc sulfide Zinc carbonate	ZnS $ZnCO_3$
Mercury	Cinnabar	Mercury(II) sulfide	HgS
Aluminum	Bauxite	Aluminum oxide	Al_2O_3
Lead	Galena	Lead(II) sulfide	PbS

potassium. Electrolysis is also used as a final stage of refining for other metals, for example, copper.

Metals that are lower down the reactivity series are bonded less vigorously as compounds, and they are separated more readily, usually by reducing them using carbon in a furnace. Zinc, iron, lead, and copper are examples of such metals.

Metals that are very low in the reactivity series have unstable compounds, and heating is sufficient to break the bonds holding them as compounds. Mercury, silver, and gold can be extracted just by heating.

Common ores

① **Rock salt**
② **Limestone**
③ **Hematite**
④ **Copper pyrites**
⑤ **Sphalerite**
⑥ **Bauxite**
⑦ **Galena**

Decomposing an oxide of a less reactive metal

The less reactive metal oxides are so low down the reactive series that they are decomposed fairly easily into the metal and oxygen just by heating.

Demonstration: heating mercury oxide

Red mercury(II) oxide (HgO) is heated in a boiling tube (①). Within a few minutes the powder turns black and begins to decompose into mercury and oxygen gas (②).

The mercury vaporizes and condenses onto the colder region near the mouth of the tube, where it forms a mercury mirror of droplets (③).

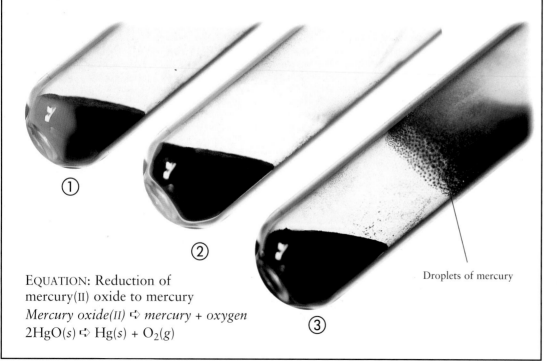

①

②

③

Droplets of mercury

EQUATION: Reduction of mercury(II) oxide to mercury

Mercury oxide(II) ⇨ *mercury + oxygen*

$2HgO(s) \Rightarrow Hg(s) + O_2(g)$

(*Above*) **The production of calcium oxide from calcium carbonate is shown on page 54.**

Decomposing an oxide of a reactive metal

It is not possible to decompose the hydroxides or oxides of the reactive metals sodium or potassium - they simply melt if heated.

Calcium hydroxide can be decomposed to its oxide and steam, but only with more energy than can be obtained easily in a laboratory. So this demonstration shows the energy involved using the reverse of the decomposition process, namely the reaction of the oxide with water.

Demonstration: hydrating calcium oxide

Some small blocks of calcium oxide (quicklime) are placed on a glass cover slip (①). Water is poured onto a few of the blocks, leaving some blocks untouched to act as a visual control.

Water reacts instantly with the calcium oxide and disappears. The reaction is very exothermic, and the reacting blocks of calcium oxide become extremely hot, swelling and giving off steam.

The blocks of reacting calcium oxide now expand and begin to crack (②). Eventually, they collapse to a dry powder, calcium hydroxide (③).

EQUATION: The formation of calcium hydroxide
Calcium oxide + water ⇨ calcium hydroxide
$CaO(s) + H_2O(l) ⇨ Ca(OH)_2(aq)$

Decomposing a metal carbonate

Most metal carbonates are insoluble in water and so cannot be extracted by dissolving them in water. The carbonates of the most reactive metals do not decompose under heating at all. The carbonates of the less reactive metals decompose more readily.

Demonstration: furnace heating of calcium carbonate

Calcium carbonate, a carbonate of a reasonably reactive metal, only decomposes at furnace temperatures. This demonstration shows the effort required to decompose a small block of calcium carbonate (limestone) to produce calcium oxide.

The furnace consists of an iron cylinder (the furnace) with a tray on which the limestone rests (①).

A cover is put over the furnace, and the limestone is heated using a Bunsen burner (②). The limestone eventually reaches a temperature at which it glows a yellow-red color (③) and gives off carbon dioxide gas. The limestone decomposes (④) to form a white solid, calcium oxide (quicklime, as shown on page 55).

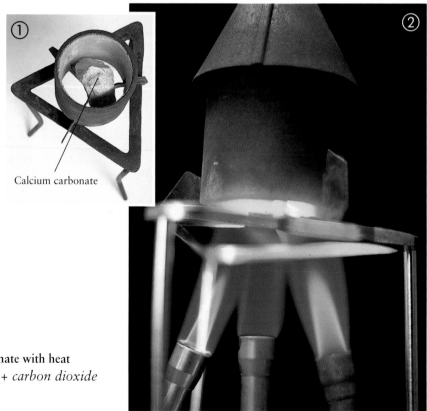

Calcium carbonate

Metal carbonate	Action of heat
Potassium carbonate	Not decomposed even at very high temperatures.
Sodium carbonate	
Calcium carbonate	Decomposed on heating into the metal oxide, releasing carbon dioxide. The ease of decomposition increases as you move down the list.
Magnesium carbonate	
Zinc carbonate	
Iron carbonate	
Lead carbonate	
Copper carbonate	Unstable — does not exist at room temperature.
Silver carbonate	

(*Above*) **Stability of metal carbonates**

EQUATION: Decomposing calcium carbonate with heat
Calcium carbonate ⇨ *calcium oxide + carbon dioxide*
$CaCO_3(s)$ ⇨ $CaO(s) + CO_2(g)$

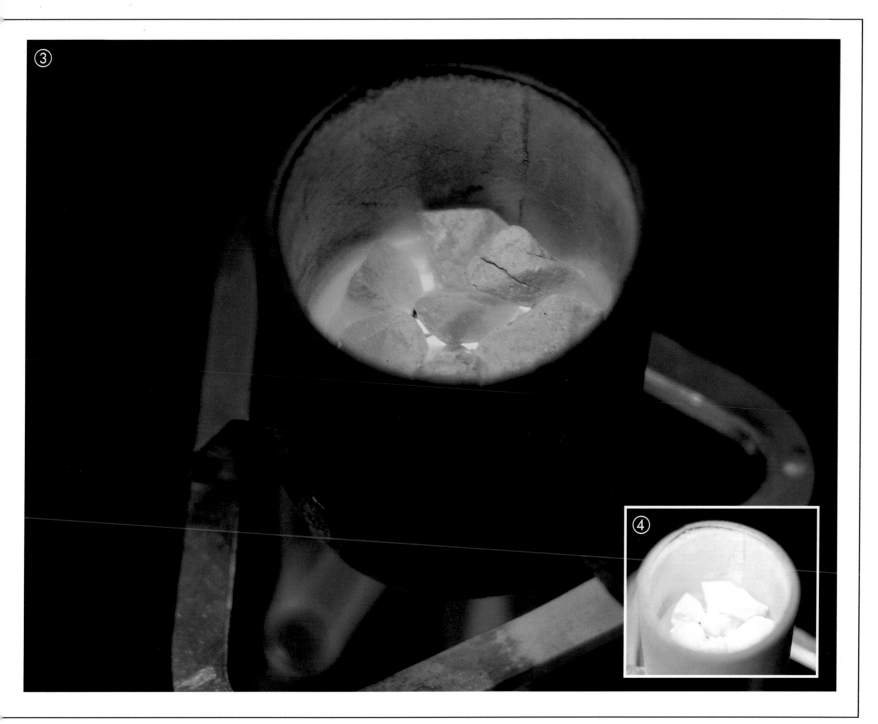

Decomposing a metal nitrate

Metal nitrates are soluble but decompose poorly. Nitrates of the reactive metals decompose on heating to produce oxygen only; those of the less reactive metals tend to release nitrogen dioxide as well as oxygen.

Demonstration: decomposing potassium nitrate

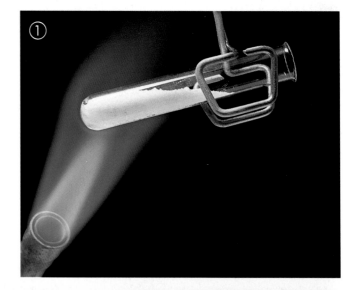

When potassium nitrate (①) is melted, it produces a greenish-yellow liquid (potassium nitrite) and gives off oxygen gas (②). Potassium nitrite is not decomposed by heating; and when the heat is removed, it eventually cools to a white solid.

The presence of oxygen is revealed by the rekindling of a glowing splint (② & ③).

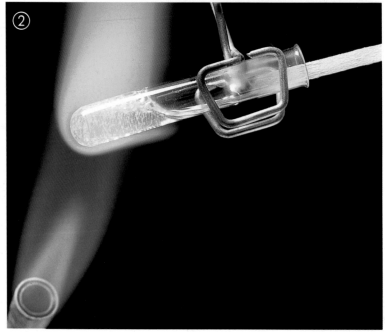

Metal nitrate	Action of heat
Potassium nitrate	When heated to a high temperature, oxygen is released. A nitrate remains, and no nitrogen dioxide is produced.
Sodium nitrate	
Calcium nitrate	Decomposed on heating to produce the metal oxide, nitrogen dioxide, and oxygen.
Magnesium nitrate	
Zinc nitrate	
Iron(II) nitrate	
Lead(II) nitrate	
Copper(II) nitrate	
Silver nitrate	Decomposed, producing the metal, oxygen, and nitrogen dioxide.

(Above) **Results of decomposing metal nitrates**

EQUATION: Decomposing potassium nitrate with heat
Potassium nitrate ⇨ potassium nitrite + oxygen
$2KNO_3(s) \Rightarrow 2KNO_2(s) + O_2(g)$

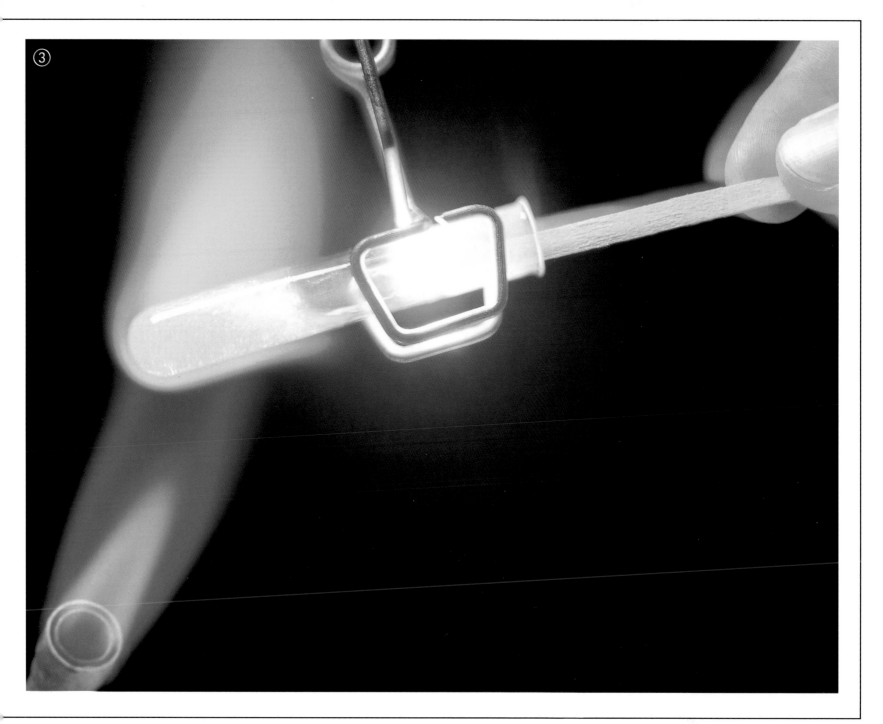

Decomposing a metal sulfide

Roasting a sulfide simply releases sulfur dioxide gas and creates an oxide, so refining has to be a two-stage process.

Copper sulfide is one of the most common metal sulfides and among the most common ores of copper. The two-stage process shown here is the basis of industrial copper smelting.

Demonstration: refining copper sulfide

This demonstration uses some copper sulfide granules. Since sulfur dioxide is a poisonous gas, this demonstration is performed in a fume chamber.

The granules are placed in a crucible lid (①). A filter paper soaked in potassium dichromate solution is used to show that no sulfur dioxide gas is released from the ore at room temperature. The copper sulfide is heated strongly with a Bunsen flame. Soon blue flames appear to dance above the copper sulfide, an indication that sulfur is being given off and is burning to produce sulfur dioxide (②). The potassium dichromate now changes to blue-green which may appear white on the paper, demonstrating that sulfur dioxide gas is being given off.

As the roasting proceeds, the red color of pure copper can be seen for a while (③); but as soon as the remaining sulfur is oxidized, the hot copper rapidly oxidizes to black copper oxide (④).

Once the oxidation of the sulfide is complete, the copper oxide is scraped off the crucible lid and into a ceramic boat (⑤), ready for the next stage (see pages 60 and 61). This final stage of smelting will be to reduce the copper oxide to copper using a reducing agent such as methane or carbon monoxide.

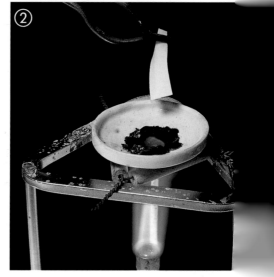

EQUATION: Reducing copper(II) sulfide

Copper(II) sulfide + oxygen from the air ⇨ copper + sulfur dioxide

$CuS(s) + O_2(g) ⇨ Cu(s) + SO_2(g)$

③

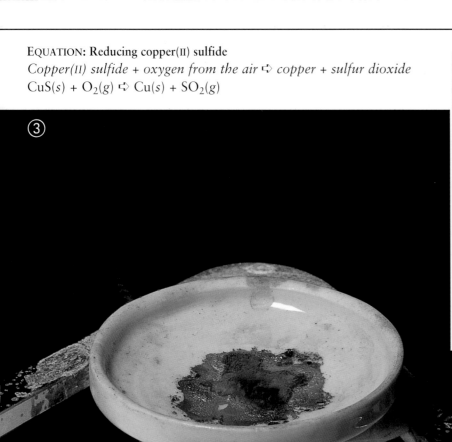

④

⑤

Tongs to hold the
hot crucible lid

Spatula

Ceramic boat

Copper oxide

Refining copper oxide

Oxides of the less reactive metals can be refined simply by reacting them with a reducing agent such as carbon monoxide.

Demonstration 1: reduction of copper oxide using carbon monoxide

The demonstration on this page shows how copper can be extracted from copper oxide using a reducing agent, in this case carbon monoxide gas, which is colorless but which burns with a characteristic blue flame. The reaction produces carbon dioxide gas, which is also colorless but does not burn. So the key to watching this sequence is to look for when the flame appears and disappears. In this way, you can tell which gas is in the tube!

Black copper oxide powder is placed in a special glass tube with a small hole near the rounded end, called a reduction tube (①). At the start the tube is full of air. This air is swept away by passing carbon monoxide gas through the tube. The carbon monoxide is lighted at the exit hole of the tube.

The tube is heated using the flame from a Bunsen burner, and the copper oxide begins to be reduced. The oxygen in the oxide combines with the carbon

monoxide to form carbon dioxide and leaves copper (②). Carbon dioxide is not flammable, so the flame at the exit hole goes out, and the copper can be seen where the powder turns a pink color.

When no further reaction is taking place between the carbon monoxide and the copper oxide, carbon monoxide once again passes out of the exit hole in the reduction tube and can be detected as it burns with a blue flame (③). The pink copper left in the tube must be allowed to cool under a continued stream of the reducing agent so that it does not oxidize back to copper oxide (④).

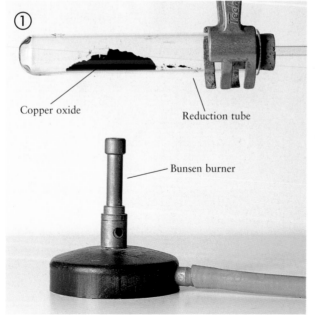

①

Copper oxide

Reduction tube

Bunsen burner

②

A similar process is used in industry, and as in this demonstration, it yields impure blocks of copper that need refining by electrolysis as shown in the second part of the demonstration.

EQUATION: Reduction of copper(II) oxide to copper

Copper(II) oxide + carbon monoxide ⇨ copper + carbon dioxide

$CuO(s) + CO(g) \Rightarrow Cu(s) + CO_2(g)$

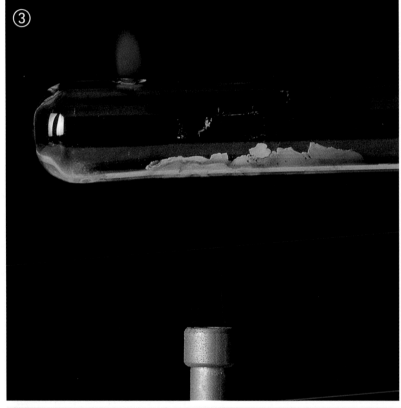

(Below) In this demonstration the copper oxide produced by the roasting of copper sulfide (as shown on pages 58 and 59) was partially reduced using methane gas as the reducing agent.

The ceramic boat containing the copper oxide is placed inside a reduction tube and heated strongly, while the reducing gas is passed through the tube. The methane is burned off as it leaves through the hole and burns continuously through the reaction because an excess is being passed through.

The picture of the boat in the bottom picture shows that some of the copper oxide has been reduced to pink copper.

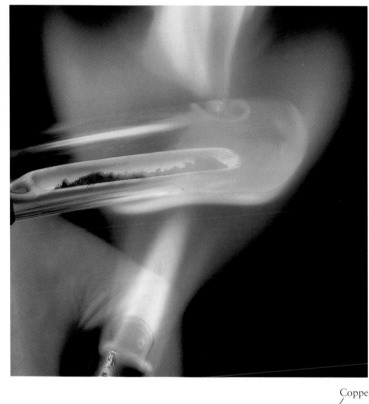

Copper

Demonstration 2: purifying copper by electrolysis

Electrolysis is a process of passing an electric current through a current-carrying solution, or electrolyte. Ions flow to the electrodes in the solution to complete a circuit in the same way as electrons flow in wires.

Deposition of copper using copper(II) sulfate as the electrolyte provides a very dramatic and easily organized demonstration of the effects of electrolysis in refining, using a laboratory power pack or low-voltage dry cells.

When a combination of copper electrodes and copper(II) sulfate is used, copper ions are formed at one electrode and transferred to the solution, while more copper ions are converted to atoms and are plated onto the other elctrode. The transfer of ions has no overall effect on the concentration of copper ions in the solution, which remains dark blue.

The apparatus consists of a glass container, some reagent quality copper(II) sulfate solution, two strips or tubes of copper, and a power pack ((①)). In this demonstration the copper strips or tubes are used as the electrodes ((②)). Two crocodile clips are used, both to make an electrical connection between the electrode and the power pack, and to fasten the electrodes to the sides of the glass. The electrodes are arranged so that they are easy to watch.

When the power pack is switched on, signs of change are evident within a minute or so ((③)). The rate of change at the electrodes depends on the current supplied by the power pack, and some experimentation is needed to get an acceptable speed of electrolysis by adjusting the voltage and the distance between the electrodes.

As the electrolysis proceeds, a change of color occurs at both electrodes. One of the electrodes soon begins to be plated in copper, and it becomes more orange colored. At the same time, the other electrode begins to look shiny simply because it is losing copper from its surface. The electrode at which deposition is occurring

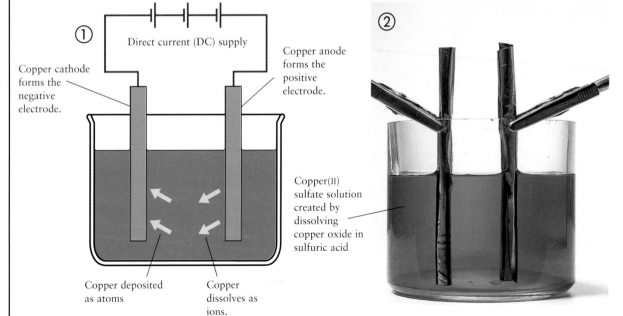

① Direct current (DC) supply

Copper cathode forms the negative electrode.

Copper anode forms the positive electrode.

Copper(II) sulfate solution created by dissolving copper oxide in sulfuric acid

Copper deposited as atoms

Copper dissolves as ions.

②

soon develops a fernlike deposit in the direction of the flow of the ions (④). This is observed most easily while the copper electrodes are still in the electrolyte, as the structure collapses as soon as they are removed (⑤).

Remarks

Notice that because some of the copper is only loosely plated and liable to fall off, any quantitative determination of the amount of copper being transferred by electrolysis is accomplished more accurately by weighing the ANODE before the demonstration and then again after the electrolysis has been under way so as to determine the loss of mass. This will be the same as the gain of mass at the CATHODE, provided that the anode is made of pure copper.

A process similar to this laboratory demonstration is used in industry to purify the copper produced from refining. In this case the anode would be the impure copper.

③

④

Fernlike deposits of copper form at the cathode.

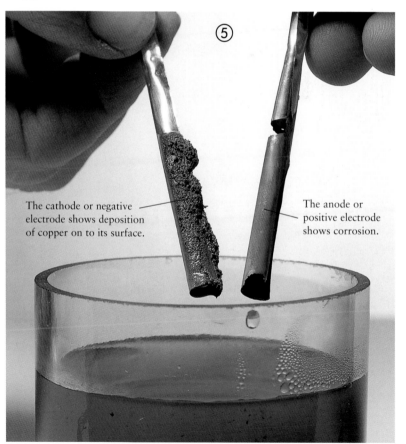

⑤

The cathode or negative electrode shows deposition of copper on to its surface.

The anode or positive electrode shows corrosion.

Refining iron ore

The oxides of the more reactive metals require strong reducing agents to reduce them to the metals. Iron oxide, or iron ore, is an oxide of a more reactive metal than copper and can be reduced only at very high temperatures, as demonstrated here.

Demonstration: reduction of iron using the Thermit process

In this demonstration a mixture of aluminum and iron oxide is placed in a glass boiling tube. At room temperature this mixture is completely unreactive. Magnesium ribbon is used as a fuse. The boiling tube and fuse are placed in a sand bath (①), and the whole apparatus is placed out in a field, well away from any inflammable materials.

The magnesium is lighted and burns with a brilliant white light. The ribbon burns down into the mixture in the boiling tube, and once sufficient heat has been released, the aluminum powder reacts with the oxygen from the iron oxide to release yet more heat (②). The reacting aluminum raises the temperature of the iron oxide to about 2000°C. The aluminum burns to form aluminum oxide, a lightweight, fine powder that is carried off easily by the rising currents of heated air (③). This is what appears as a white smoke.

The iron oxide is reduced to molten iron, a heavy liquid, that forms a pool in the sand together with the molten glass from the boiling tube (④).

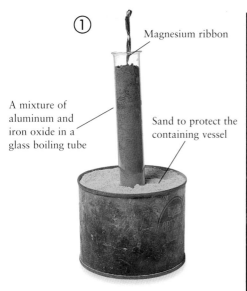

①

Magnesium ribbon

A mixture of aluminum and iron oxide in a glass boiling tube

Sand to protect the containing vessel

②

③

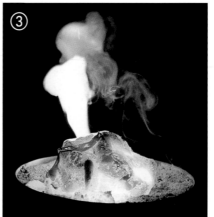

Remarks

Because this demonstration produces temperatures in excess of 2000°C, it was performed outside a laboratory on open ground and with no spectators nearby. The qualified demonstrator and photographer used suitable protective clothing.

EQUATION: Reduction of iron(III) oxide to iron
Iron(III) oxide + aluminum ⇨ iron + aluminum oxide
$Fe_2O_3(s) + 2Al(s) \Rightarrow 2Fe(s) + Al_2O_3(s)$
Heat

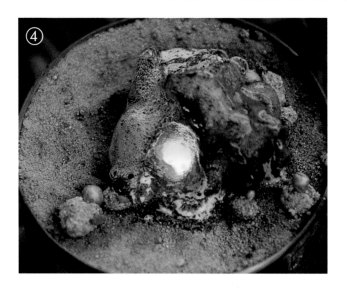

Iron-making: the blast furnace

A blast furnace is a tall oven in which the conditions are controlled so that the iron ORE (iron(III) oxide) entering the top is reduced progressively (oxygen is removed) to iron metal that flows to the bottom.

Modern blast furnaces are designed to run continuously. They are charged with a mixture of iron ore, coke, and limestone at the top of the furnace. Each ton of iron uses up about three-quarters of a ton of coke and a quarter of a ton of limestone.

The smelting process

Essentially, the furnace has to remove the oxygen from the metal ore (the ore must be reduced) and then keep any waste rock separated from the molten iron. This is done with a very hot blast of carbon monoxide gas.

The whole furnace is designed so that hot carbon monoxide gas is produced continuously and blown through melting rock. Carbon monoxide gas is produced at the bottom of the furnace in a two-stage process. First, air is blown into the bottom of the furnace, and the coke, which is almost entirely carbon, is oxidized with the oxygen from the air to produce carbon dioxide gas, a reaction that also gives out heat.

As the carbon dioxide bubbles up the furnace, it reacts with more of the coke in the mixture, being reduced to carbon monoxide gas. This is the gas that reacts with the iron ore (usually iron oxide) in the middle of the furnace, reducing it, in turn, to yield liquid iron.

Iron and waste materials (SLAG) separate as they melt and are drawn off from the bottom of the furnace.

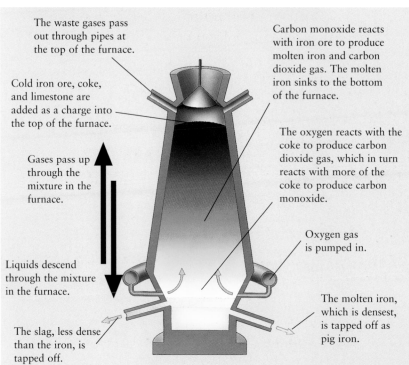

The waste gases pass out through pipes at the top of the furnace.

Cold iron ore, coke, and limestone are added as a charge into the top of the furnace.

Gases pass up through the mixture in the furnace.

Liquids descend through the mixture in the furnace.

The slag, less dense than the iron, is tapped off.

Carbon monoxide reacts with iron ore to produce molten iron and carbon dioxide gas. The molten iron sinks to the bottom of the furnace.

The oxygen reacts with the coke to produce carbon dioxide gas, which in turn reacts with more of the coke to produce carbon monoxide.

Oxygen gas is pumped in.

The molten iron, which is densest, is tapped off as pig iron.

EQUATION: Oxidation of coke
Carbon + oxygen ⇨ carbon dioxide
$C(s) + O_2(g) \Rightarrow CO_2(g)$

EQUATION: Reduction of carbon dioxide
Carbon dioxide + carbon ⇨ carbon monoxide
$CO_2(g) + C(s) \Rightarrow 2CO(s)$

EQUATION: Reduction of iron(III) oxide
Iron(III) oxide + carbon monoxide ⇨ iron metal + carbon dioxide
$Fe_2O_3(s) + 3CO(g) \Rightarrow 2Fe(l) + 3CO_2(g)$

MASTER GLOSSARY

absolute zero: the lowest possible temperature (−273.15°C).

absorption: the process by which a substance is soaked up. *See:* adsorption.

acid: a substance that can give a proton to another substance. Acids are compounds containing hydrogen that can attack and dissolve many substances. Acids are described as weak or strong, dilute or concentrated, mineral or organic. *Example:* hydrochloric acid (HCl). An acid in water can react with a base to form a salt and water.

acidic solution: a solution with a pH lower than 7. *See:* pH.

acidity: a general term for the strength of an acid in a solution.

acid radical: the negative ion left behind when an acid loses a hydrogen ion. *Example:* Cl⁻ in hydrochloric acid (HCl).

acid salt: An ACID SALT contains at least one hydrogen ion and can behave as an acid in chemical reactions. Acid salts are produced under conditions that do not allow complete neutralization of the acid. For example, sulfuric acid may react with a sodium compound to produce a normal sodium salt, sodium sulfate (Na_2SO_4), or it may retain some of the hydrogen, in which case it becomes the salt sodium hydrogen sulfate ($NaHSO_4$).

actinide series or actinide metals: a series of 15 similar radioactive elements between actinium and lawrencium. They are transition metals.

activated charcoal: a form of carbon made of tiny crystals of graphite that is made by heating organic matter in the absence of air. It is then further processed to increase its pore space and therefore its surface area. Its surface area is about 2000 m^2/g. Activated charcoal readily adsorbs many gases, and it is therefore widely used as a filter, for example, in gas masks.

activation energy: the energy required to make a reaction occur. The greater the activation energy of a reaction, the more its reaction rate depends on temperature. The activation energy of a reaction is useful because, if the rate of reaction is known at one temperature (for example, 100 °C) then the activation energy can be used to calculate the rate of reaction at another temperature (for example, at 400 °C) without actually doing the experiment.

adsorption: the process by which a surface adsorbs a substance. The substances involved are not chemically combined and can be separated. *See:* absorption.

alchemy: the traditional "art" of working with chemicals common in the Middle Ages. One of the main challenges for alchemists was to make gold from lead. Alchemy faded away as scientific chemistry was developed in the 17th century.

alcohol: an organic compound that contains a hydroxyl (OH) group. *Example:* ethanol (CH_3CH_2OH), also known as ethyl alcohol or grain alcohol.

alkali/alkaline: a base in (aqueous) solution. Alkalis react with or neutralize hydrogen ions in acids and have a pH greater than 7.0 because they contain relatively few hydrogen ions. *Example:* aqueous sodium hydroxide (NaOH). *See:* pH.

alkaline cell (or battery): a dry cell in which the electrolyte contains sodium or potassium hydroxide.

alkaline earth metal: a member of Group 2 of the Periodic Table. *Example:* calcium.

alkali metals: a member of Group 1 of the Periodic Table. *Example:* sodium.

alkane: a hydrocarbon with no carbon-to-carbon multiple bonds. *Example:* ethane, C_2H_6.

alkene: a hydrocarbon with at least one carbon-to-carbon double bond. *Example:* ethylene, C_2H_4.

alkyne: a hydrocarbon with at least one carbon-to-carbon triple bond. *Example:* acetylene, C_2H_2.

allotropes: alternative forms of an element that differ in the way the atoms are linked. *Example:* white and red phosphorus.

alloy: a mixture of a metal and various other elements. *Example:* brass is an alloy of copper and zinc.

amalgam: a liquid alloy of mercury with another metal.

amorphous: a solid in which the atoms are not arranged regularly (i.e., "glassy"). Compare crystalline.

amphoteric: a metal that will react with both acids and alkalis. *Example:* aluminum metal.

anhydrous: lacking water; water has been removed, for example by heating. (Opposite of anhydrous is hydrous or hydrated.) *Example:* copper(II) sulfate can be anhydrous ($CuSO_4$) or hydrated ($CuSO_4 \bullet 5H_2O$).

anion: a negatively charged atom or group of atoms. *Examples*: chloride ion (Cl⁻), hydroxide ion (OH⁻). *See:* pH.

anode: the electrode at which oxidation occurs; the negative terminal of a battery or the positive electrode of an electrolysis cell.

anodizing: a process that uses the effect of electrolysis to make a surface corrosion-resistant. *Example:* anodized aluminum.

antacid: a common name for any compound that reacts with stomach acid to neutralize it. *Example:* sodium hydrogen carbonate, also known as sodium bicarbonate.

antioxidant: a substance that reacts rapidly with radicals, thereby preventing oxidation of some other substance.

antibumping granules: small glass or ceramic beads designed to promote boiling without the development of large gas bubbles.

approximate relative atomic mass: *See:* relative atomic mass.

aqueous: a solution in which the solvent is water. Usually used as "aqueous solution." *Example:* aqueous solution of sodium hydroxide (NaOH(*aq*)).

aromatic hydrocarbons: compounds of carbon that have the benzene ring as part of their structure. *Examples:* benzene (C_6H_6), naphthalene ($C_{10}H_8$). They are known as aromatic because of their strong pungent smell.

atmospheric pressure: the pressure exerted by the gases in the air. Units of measurement are kilopascals (kPa), atmospheres (atm), millimeters of mercury (mm Hg), and Torr. Standard atmospheric pressure is 100 kPa, 1atm, 760 mm Hg or 760 Torr.

atom: the smallest particle of an element; a nucleus and its surrounding electrons.

atomic mass: the mass of an atom measured in atomic mass units (u). An atomic mass unit equals one twelfth of the atom of carbon-12.

"Atomic mass" is now more generally used than "atomic weight." *Example:* the atomic mass of chlorine is about 35 u. *See:* atomic weight, relative atomic mass.

atomic number: also known as proton number. The number of electrons or the number of protons in an atom. *Example:* the atomic number of gold is 79.

atomic structure: the nucleus and the arrangement of electrons around it.

atomic weight: a common term used to mean the average molar mass of an element (g/mol). This is the mass per mole of atoms. *Example:* the atomic weight of chlorine is about 35 g/mol. *See:* atomic mass, mole.

base: a substance that can accept a proton from another substance. *Example:* aqueous ammonia ($NH_3(aq)$). A base can react with an acid in water to form a salt and water.

basic salt: a salt that contains at least one hydroxide ion. The hydroxide ion can then behave as a base in chemical reactions. *Example:* the reaction of hydrochloric acid (HCl) with the base aluminum hydroxide ($Al(OH)_3$) can form two basic salts, $Al(OH)_2Cl$ and $Al(OH)Cl_2$.

battery: a number of electrochemical cells placed in series.

bauxite: a hydrated impure oxide of aluminum ($Al_2O_3 \bullet xH_2O$, with the amount of water x being variable). It is the main ore used to obtain aluminum metal. The reddish brown color of bauxite is mainly caused by the iron oxide impurities it contains.

beehive shelf: an inverted earthenware bowl with a hole in the upper surface and a slot in the rim. Traditionally the earthenware was brown and looked similar to a beehive, hence its name. A delivery tube passes through the slot, and a gas jar is placed over the hole. This provides a convenient way to collect gas over water in a pneumatic trough.

bell jar: a tall glass jar with an open bottom and a wide, stoppered neck that is used in conjunction with a beehive shelf and a pneumatic trough in some experiments involving gases. The name derives from historic versions of the apparatus, which resembled a bell in shape.

blast furnace: a tall furnace charged with a mixture of iron ore, coke, and limestone and used for the refining of iron metal. The name comes from the strong blast of air introduced during smelting.

bleach: a substance that removes color from stains on materials either by oxidizing or reducing the staining compound. *Example:* sulfur dioxide (SO_2).

block: one of the main divisions of the Periodic Table. Blocks are named for the outermost occupied electron shell of an element. *Example:* the Transition Metals all belong to the d-block.

boiling point: the temperature at which a liquid boils, changing from a liquid to a gas. Boiling points change with atmospheric pressure. *Example:* The boiling point of pure water at standard atmospheric pressure is 100 °C.

boiling tube: A thin glass tube closed at one end and used for chemical tests. The composition and thickness of the glass is such that it cannot sustain very high temperatures and is intended for heating liquids to boiling point. *See:* side-arm boiling tube, test tube.

bond: chemical bonding is either a transfer or sharing of electrons by two or more atoms. There are a number of types of chemical bond, some very strong (such as covalent and ionic bonds), others weak (such as hydrogen bonds). Chemical bonds form because the linked molecule is more stable than the unlinked atoms from which it formed. *Example:* the hydrogen molecule (H_2) is more stable than single atoms of hydrogen, which is why hydrogen gas is always found as molecules of two hydrogen atoms.

Boyle's Law: At constant temperature, and for a given mass of gas, the volume of the gas (V) is inversely proportional to pressure that builds up (P): $P \propto 1/V$.

brine: a solution of salt (sodium chloride, NaCl) in water.

Büchner flask: a thick-walled side-arm flask designed to withstand the changes in pressure that occur when the flask is connected to a suction pump.

Büchner funnel: a special design of plastic or ceramic funnel that has a flat stage on which a filter paper can be placed. It is intended for use under suction with a Büchner funnel.

buffer (solution): a mixture of substances in solution that resists a change in the acidity or alkalinity of the solution when small amounts of an acid or alkali are added.

burette: a long, graduated glass tube with a tap at one end. A burette is used vertically, with the tap lowermost, as a reservoir for a chemical during titration.

burn: a combustion reaction in which a flame is produced. A flame occurs where *gases* combust and release heat and light. At least two gases are therefore required if there is to be a flame. *Example:* methane gas (CH_4) burns in oxygen gas (O_2) to produce carbon dioxide (CO_2) and water (H_2O) and give out heat and light.

calorimeter: an insulated container designed to prevent heat gain or loss with the environment and thus allow changes of temperature within reacting chemicals to be measured accurately. It is named after the old unit of heat, the calorie.

capillary: a very small diameter (glass) tube. Capillary tubing has a small enough diameter to allow surface tension effects to retain water within the tube.

capillary action: the tendency for a liquid to be sucked into small spaces, such as between objects and through narrow-pore tubes. The force to do this comes from surface tension.

carbohydrate: a compound containing only carbon, hydrogen and oxygen. Carbohydrates have the formula $C_n(H_2O)_n$, where n is variable. *Example:* glucose ($C_6H_{12}O_6$).

carbonate: a salt of carbonic acid. Carbonate ions have the chemical formula CO_3^{2-}. *Examples:* calcium nitrate $CaCO_3$ and sodium carbonate Na_2CO_3.

catalyst: a substance that speeds up a chemical reaction but itself remains unaltered at the end of the reaction. *Example:* copper in the reaction of hydrochloric acid with zinc.

catalytic converter: a device incorporated into some exhaust systems. The catalytic converter contains a framework or granules with a very large surface area and coated with catalysts that convert the pollutant gases passing over them into harmless products.

cathode: the electrode at which reduction occurs; the positive terminal of a battery or the negative electrode of an electrolysis cell.

cathodic protection: the technique of protecting a metal object by connecting it to a more readily oxidizable metal. The metal object being protected is made into the cathode of a cell. *Example:* iron can be protected by coupling it with magnesium. Iron forms the cathode and magnesium the anode.

cation: a positively charged ion. *Examples:* calcium ion (Ca^{2+}), ammonium ion (NH_4^+).

caustic: a substance that can cause burns if it touches the skin. *Example:* Sodium hydroxide, caustic soda (NaOH).

Celsius scale (°C): a temperature scale on which the freezing point of water is at 0 degrees, and the normal boiling point at standard atmospheric pressure is 100 degrees.

cell: a vessel containing two electrodes and an electrolyte that can act as an electrical conductor.

centrifuge: an instrument for spinning small samples very rapidly. The fast spin makes the components of a mixture that have a different density separate, as in filtration.

ceramic: a material based on clay minerals that has been heated so that it has chemically hardened.

chalcogens: the members of Group 6 of the Periodic Table: oxygen, sulfur, selenium and tellurium. The word comes from the Greek meaning "brass giver," because all these elements are found in copper ores, and copper is the most important metal in making brass.

change of state: a change between two of the three states of matter, solid, liquid, and gas. *Example:* when water evaporates it changes from a liquid to a gaseous state.

Charles's Law: The volume (V) of a given mass of gas at constant pressure is directly proportional to its absolute temperature (T): $V \propto T$.

chromatography: A separation technique uses the ability of surfaces to adsorb substances with different strengths. The substances with the least adherence to the surface move faster and leave behind those that adhere more strongly.

coagulation: a term describing the tendency of small particles to stick together in clumps.

coherent: meaning that a substance holds together or sticks together well, and without holes or other defects. *Example:* Aluminum appears unreactive because, as soon as new metal is exposed to air, it forms a very complete oxide coating, which then stops further reaction occurring.

coinage metals: the elements copper, silver, and gold, used to make coins.

coke: a solid substance left after the gases have been extracted from coal.

colloid: a mixture of ultramicroscopic particles dispersed uniformly through a second substance to form a suspension that may be almost like a solution or may set to a jelly (gel). The word comes from the Greek for glue.

colorimeter: an instrument for measuring the light-absorbing power of a substance. The absorption gives an accurate indication of the concentration of some colored solutions.

combustion: a reaction in which an element or compound is oxidized to release energy. Some combustion reactions are slow, such as the combustion of the sugar we eat to provide energy. If the combustion results in a flame, it is called burning. A flame occurs where *gases* combust and release heat and light. At least two gases are therefore required if there is to be a flame. *Example:* the combustion or burning of methane gas (CH_4) in oxygen gas (O_2) produces carbon dioxide (CO_2)

and water (H_2O) and gives out heat and light. Some combustion reactions produce light and heat but do not produce flames. *Example:* the combustion of carbon in oxygen produces an intense red-white light but no flame.

combustion spoon: also known as a deflagrating spoon, it consists of a long metal handle with a small cup at the end. Its purpose is to allow the safe introduction of a (usually heated) substance into a filled gas jar, when the reaction is likely to be vigorous. *Example:* the introduction of a heated sodium pellet into a gas jar containing chlorine.

compound: a chemical consisting of two or more elements chemically bonded together. *Example:* Calcium atoms can combine with carbon atoms and oxygen atoms to make calcium carbonate ($CaCO_3$), a compound of all three atoms.

condensation: the formation of a liquid from a gas. This is a change of state, also called a phase change.

condensation nuclei: microscopic particles of dust, salt, and other materials suspended in the air that attract water molecules. The usual result is the formation of water droplets.

condensation polymer: a polymer formed by a chain of reactions in which a water molecule is eliminated as every link of the polymer is formed. *Examples:* polyesters, proteins, nylon.

conduction: (i) the exchange of heat (heat conduction) by contact with another object, or (ii) allowing the flow of electrons (electrical conduction).

conductivity: the ability of a substance to conduct. The conductivity of a solution depends on there being suitable free ions in the solution. A conducting solution is called an electrolyte. *Example:* dilute sulfuric acid.

convection: the exchange of heat energy with the surroundings produced by the flow of a fluid due to being heated or cooled.

corrosion: the oxidation of a metal. Corrosion is often regarded as unwanted and is more generally used to refer to the *slow* decay of a metal resulting from contact with gases and liquids in the environment. *Example:* Rust is the corrosion of iron.

corrosive: causing corrosion. *Example:* Sodium hydroxide (NaOH).

covalent bond: this is the most common form of strong chemical bonding and occurs when two atoms *share* electrons. *Example:* oxygen (O_2)

cracking: breaking down complex molecules into simpler compounds, as in oil refining.

crucible: a small bowl with a lip, made of heat-resistant white glazed ceramic. It is used for heating substances using a Bunsen flame.

crude oil: a chemical mixture of petroleum liquids. Crude oil forms the raw material for an oil refinery.

crystal: a substance that has grown freely so that it can develop external faces. Compare with crystalline, where the atoms are not free to form individual crystals, and amorphous, where the atoms are arranged irregularly.

crystalline: a solid in which the atoms, ions, or molecules are organized into an orderly pattern without distinct crystal faces. *Examples:* copper(II) sulfate, sodium chloride. Compare amorphous.

crystallization: the process in which a solute comes out of solution slowly and forms crystals. *See:* water of crystallization.

crystal systems: seven patterns or systems into which all crystals can be grouped: cubic, hexagonal, rhombohedral, tetragonal, orthorhombic, monoclinic, and triclinic.

cubic crystal system: groupings of crystals that look like cubes.

current: an electric current is produced by a flow of electrons through a conducting solid or ions through a conducting liquid. The rate of supply of this charge is measured in amperes (A).

decay (radioactive decay): the way that a radioactive element changes into another element due to loss of mass through radiation. *Example:* uranium 238 decays with the loss of an alpha particle to form thorium 234.

decomposition: the break down of a substance (for example, by heat or with the aid of a catalyst) into simpler components. In such a chemical reaction only one substance is involved. *Example:* hydrogen peroxide ($H_2O_2(aq)$) into oxygen ($O_2(g)$) and water ($H_2O(l)$).

decrepitation: when, as part of the decomposition of a substance, cracking sounds are also produced. *Example:* heating of lead nitrate ($Pb(NO_3)_2$).

dehydration: the removal of water from a substance by heating it, placing it in a dry atmosphere, or using a drying (dehydrating) reagent such as concentrated sulfuric acid.

density: the mass per unit volume (e.g., g/cc).

desalinization: the removal of all the salts from sea water, by reverse osmosis or heating the water and collecting the distillate. It is a very energy-intensive process.

desiccant: a substance that absorbs water vapor from the air. *Example:* silica gel.

desiccator: a lidded glass bowl containing a shelf. The apparatus is designed to store materials in dry air. A desiccant is placed below the shelf, and the substance to be dried is placed on the shelf. The lid makes a gas-tight joint with the bowl.

destructive distillation: the heating of a material so that it decomposes entirely to release all of its volatile components. Destructive distillation is also known as pyrolysis.

detergent: a chemical based on petroleum that removes dirt.

Devarda's alloy: zinc with a trace of copper that acts as a catalyst for reactions with the zinc.

diaphragm: a semipermeable membrane – a kind of ultrafine mesh filter – that allows only small ions to pass through. It is used in the electrolysis of brine.

diffusion: the slow mixing of one substance with another until the two substances are evenly mixed. Mixing occurs because of differences in concentration within the mixture. Diffusion works rapidly with gases, very slowly with liquids.

diffusion combustion: the form of combustion that occurs when two gases just begin to mix during ignition. As a result, the flame is hollow and yellow in color. *Example:* a candle flame.

dilute acid: an acid whose concentration has been reduced in a large proportion of water.

disinfectant: a chemical that kills bacteria and other microorganisms.

displacement reaction: a reaction that occurs because metals differ in their reactivity. If a more reactive metal is placed in a solution of a less reactive metal compound, a reaction occurs in which the more reactive metal displaces the metal ions in the solution. *Example:* when zinc metal is introduced into a solution of copper(II) sulfate (which thus supplies copper ions), zinc goes into solution as zinc ions, while copper is displaced from the solution and forced to precipitate as metallic copper.

dissociate: to break bonds apart. In the case of acids it means to break up forming hydrogen ions. This is an example of ionization. Strong acids dissociate completely. Weak acids are not completely ionized, and a solution of a weak acid has a relatively low concentration of hydrogen ions.

dissolve: to break down a substance in a solution without causing a reaction.

distillation: the process of separating mixtures by condensing the vapors through cooling.

distilled water: distilled water is nearly pure water and is produced by distillation of tap water. Distilled water is used in the laboratory in preference to tap water because the distillation process removes many of the impurities in tap water that may influence the chemical reactions for which the water is used.

Dreschel bottle: a tall bottle with a special stopper designed to allow a gas to pass through a liquid. The stopper contains both inlet and outlet tubes. One tube extends below the surface of the liquid so that the gas has to pass through the liquid before it can escape to the outlet tube.

dropper funnel: a special funnel with a tap to allow the controlled release of a liquid. Also known as a dropping funnel or tap funnel.

drying agent: *See:* dehydrating agent.

dye: a colored substance that will stick to another substance so that both appear colored.

effervesce: to give off bubbles of gas.

effloresce: to lose water and turn to a fine powder on exposure to the air. *Example:* Sodium carbonate on the rim of a reagent bottle stopper.

electrical conductivity: *See:* conductivity

electrical potential: the energy produced by an electrochemical cell and measured by the voltage or electromotive force (emf). *See:* potential difference, electromotive force.

electrochemical cell: a cell consisting of two electrodes and an electrolyte. It can be set up to generate an electric current (usually known as a galvanic cell, an example of which is a battery), or an electric current can be passed through it to produce a chemical reaction (in which case it is called an electrolytic cell and can be used to refine metals or for electroplating).

electrochemical series: the arrangement of substances that are either oxidizing or reducing agents in order of strength as a reagent, for example, with the strong oxidizing agents at the top of the list and the strong reducing agents at the bottom.

electrode: a conductor that forms one terminal of a cell.

electrolysis: an electrical-chemical process that uses an electric current to cause the breakup of a compound and the movement of metal ions in a solution. The process happens in many natural situations (as for example in rusting) and is also commonly used in industry for purifying (refining) metals or for plating metal objects with a fine, even metal coating.

electrolyte: an ionic solution that conducts electricity.

electrolytic cell: *See:* electrochemical cell

electromotive force (emf): the force set up in an electric circuit by a potential difference.

electron: a tiny, negatively charged particle that is part of an atom. The flow of electrons through a solid material such as a wire produces an electric current.

electron configuration: the pattern in which electrons are arranged in shells around the nucleus of an atom. *Example:* chlorine has the configuration 2, 8, 7.

electroplating: depositing a thin layer of a metal onto the surface of another substance using electrolysis.

element: a substance that cannot be decomposed into simpler substance by chemical means. *Examples:* calcium, iron, gold.

emulsion: tiny droplets of one substance dispersed in another. One common oil in water emulsion is called milk. Because the tiny droplets tend to come together, another stabilizing substance is often needed. Soaps and detergents are such agents, wrapping the particles of grease and oil in a stable coat. Photographic film is an example of a solid emulsion.

endothermic reaction: a reaction that takes in heat. *Example:* when ammonium chloride is dissolved in water.

end point: the stage in a titration when the reaction between the titrant (added from a burette) and the titrate (in the flask) is complete. The end point is normally recognized by use of an indicator that has been added to the titrate. In an acid-base reaction this is also called the neutralization point.

enzyme: biological catalysts in the form of proteins in the body that speed up chemical reactions. Every living cell contains hundreds of enzymes that help the processes of life continue.

ester: organic compounds formed by the reaction of an alcohol with an acid and which often have a fruity taste. *Example:* ethyl acetate ($CH_3COOC_2H_5$).

evaporation: the change of state of a liquid to a gas. Evaporation happens below the boiling point and is used as a method of separating the materials in a solution.

excess, to: if a reactant has been added to another reactant in excess, it has exceeded the amount required to complete the reaction.

exothermic reaction: a reaction that gives out substantial amounts of heat. *Example:* sucrose and concentrated sulfuric acid.

explosive: a substance that, when a shock is applied to it, decomposes very rapidly, releasing a very large amount of heat and creating a large volume of gases as a shock wave.

fat: semisolid, energy-rich compounds derived from plants or animals, made of carbon, hydrogen, and oxygen.

ferment: to break down a substance by microorganisms in the absence of oxygen. *Example:* fermentation of sugar to ethyl alcohol during the production of alcoholic drinks.

filtrate: the liquid that has passed through a filter.

filtration: the separation of a liquid from a solid using a membrane with small holes (i.e. a filter paper).

flame: a mixture of gases undergoing burning. A solid or liquid must produce a gas before it can react with oxygen and burn with a flame.

flammable (also inflammable): able to burn (in air). *Opposite:* nonflammable.

flocculation: the grouping together of small particles in a suspension to form particles large enough to settle out as a precipitate. Flocculation is usually caused by the presence of a flocculating agent. *Example:* calcium ions are the flocculating agent for suspended clay particles.

fluid: able to flow; either a liquid or a gas.

fluorescent: a substance that gives out visible light when struck by invisible waves, such as ultraviolet rays.

flux: a material used to make it easier for a liquid to flow. A flux dissolves metal oxides and so prevents a metal from oxidizing while being heated.

foam: a substance that is sufficiently gelatinous to be able to contain bubbles of gas. The gas bulks up the substance, making it behave as though it were semirigid.

fossil fuels: hydrocarbon compounds that have been formed from buried plant and animal remains. High pressures and temperatures lasting over millions of years are required. *Examples:* The fossil fuels are coal, oil and natural gas.

fraction: a group of similar components of a mixture. *Example:* In the petroleum industry the light fractions of crude oil are those with the smallest molecules, while the medium and heavy fractions have larger molecules.

fractional distillation: the separation of the components of a liquid mixture by heating them to their boiling points.

fractionating column: a glass column designed to allow different fractions to be separated when they boil. In industry it may be called a fractionating tower.

free radical: a very reactive atom or group with a "spare" electron. *Example:* methyl, $CH_3\bullet$.

freezing point: the temperature at which a substance undergoes a phase change from a liquid to a solid. It is the same temperature as the melting point.

fuel: a concentrated form of chemical energy. The main sources of fuels (called fossil fuels because

they were formed by geological processes) are coal, crude oil, and natural gas.

fuel rods: the rods of uranium or other radioactive material used as a fuel in nuclear power plants.

fume chamber or fume cupboard: a special laboratory chamber fitted with a protective glass shield and containing a powerful extraction fan to remove toxic fumes.

fuming: an unstable liquid that gives off a gas. Very concentrated acid solutions are often fuming solutions. *Example:* fuming nitric acid.

galvanizing: applying a thin zinc coating to protect another metal.

gamma rays: waves of radiation produced as the nucleus of a radioactive element rearranges itself into a tighter cluster of protons and neutrons. Gamma rays carry enough energy to damage living cells.

gangue: the unwanted material in an ore.

gas/gaseous phase: a form of matter in which the molecules form no definite shape and are free to move about to uniformly fill any vessel they are put in. A gas can easily be compressed into a much smaller volume.

gas syringe: a glass syringe with a graduated cylinder designed to collect and measure small amounts of gases produced during an experiment.

gelatinous precipitate: a precipitate that has a jelly-like appearance. *Example:* iron (III) hydroxide. Because a gelatinous precipitate is mostly water, it is of a similar density to water and will float or lie suspended in the liquid. *See:* granular precipitate.

glass: a transparent silicate without any crystal growth. It has a glassy luster and breaks with a curved fracture. Note that some minerals have all these features and are therefore natural glasses. Household glass is a synthetic silicate.

glucose: the most common of the natural sugars ($C_6H_{12}O_6$). It occurs as the polymer known as cellulose, the fiber in plants. Starch is also a form of glucose.

granular precipitate: a precipitate that has a grainlike appearance. *Example:* lead(II) hydroxide. *See:* gelatinous precipitate.

gravimetric analysis: a quantitative form of analysis in which the mass (weight) of the reactants and products is measured.

group: a vertical column in the Periodic Table. There are eight groups in the table. Their numbers correspond to the number of electrons in the outer shell of the atoms in the group. *Example:* Group 1: member, sodium.

Greenhouse Effect: an increase in the global air temperature as a result of heat released from burning fossil fuels being absorbed by carbon dioxide in the atmosphere.

Greenhouse gas: any of various gases that contribute to the Greenhouse Effect. *Example:* carbon dioxide.

half-life: the time it takes for the radiation coming from a sample of a radioactive element to decrease by half.

halide: a salt of one of the halogens.

halogen: one of a group of elements including chlorine, bromine, iodine, and fluorine in Group 7 of the Periodic Table.

heat: the energy that is transferred when a substance is at a different temperature than its surroundings. *See:* endothermic and exothermic reactions.

heat capacity: the ratio of the heat supplied to a substance compared to the rise in temperature that is produced.

heat of combustion: the amount of heat given off by a mole of a substance during combustion. This heat is a property of the substance and is the same no matter what kind of combustion is involved. *Example:* heat of combustion of carbon is 94.05 kcal (x 4.18 = 393.1 kJ).

hydrate: a solid compound in crystalline form that contains water molecules. Hydrates commonly form when a solution of a soluble salt is evaporated. The water that forms part of a hydrate crystal is known as the "water of crystallization." It can usually be removed by heating, leaving an anhydrous salt.

hydration: the process of absorption of water by a substance. In some cases hydration makes the substance change color; in many other cases there is no color change, simply a change in volume. *Example:* dark blue hydrated copper(II) sulfate ($CuSO_4•5H_2O$) can be heated to produce white anhydrous copper(II) sulfate ($CuSO_4$).

hydride: a compound containing just hydrogen and another element, most often a metal. *Examples:* water (H_2O), methane (CH_4) and phosphine (PH_3).

hydrous: hydrated with water. *See:* anhydrous.

hydrocarbon: a compound in which only hydrogen and carbon atoms are present. Most fuels are hydrocarbons, as is the simple plastic polyethylene. *Example:* methane CH_4.

hydrogen bond: a type of attractive force that holds one molecule to another. It is one of the weaker forms of intermolecular attractive force. *Example:* hydrogen bonds occur in water.

ignition temperature: the temperature at which a substance begins to burn.

immiscible: will not mix with another substance. e.g., oil and water.

incandescent: glowing or shining with heat. *Example:* tungsten filament in an incandescent light bulb.

incomplete combustion: combustion in which only some of the reactant or reactants combust, or the products are not those that would be obtained if all the reactions went to completion. It is uncommon for combustion to be complete, and incomplete combustion is more frequent. *Example:* incomplete combustion of carbon in oxygen produces carbon monoxide and not carbon dioxide.

indicator (acid-base indicator): a substance or mixture of substances used to test the acidity or alkalinity of a substance. An indicator changes color depending on the acidity of the solution being tested. Many indicators are complicated organic substances. Some indicators used in the laboratory include Universal Indicator, litmus, phenolphthalein, methyl orange and bromothymol. *See:* Universal Indicator.

induction period: the time taken for a reaction to reach ignition temperature. During this period no apparent reaction occurs; then the materials appear to undergo spontaneous combustion.

inert: unreactive.

inhibitor: a substance that prevents a reaction from occurring.

inorganic substance: a substance that does not contain carbon and hydrogen. Examples: NaCl, $CaCO_3$.

insoluble: a substance that will not dissolve.

ion: an atom, or group of atoms, that has gained or lost one or more electrons and so developed an electrical charge. Ions behave differently than electrically neutral atoms and molecules. They can move in an electric field, and they can also bind strongly to solvent molecules such as water. Positively charged ions are called cations; negatively charged ions are called anions. Ions can carry an electrical current through solutions.

ionic bond: the form of bonding that occurs between two ions when the ions have opposite charges. *Example:* sodium cations bond with chloride anions to form common salt (NaCl) when a salty solution is evaporated. Ionic bonds are strong bonds except in the presence of a solvent. *See:* bond.

ionic compound: a compound that consists of ions. *Example:* NaCl.

ionize: to break up neutral molecules into oppositely charged ions or to convert atoms into ions by the loss of electrons.

ionization: a process that creates ions.

isotope: an atom that has the same number of protons in its nucleus, but which has a different mass. *Example:* carbon 12 and carbon 14.

Kipp's apparatus: a piece of glassware consisting of three chambers, designed to provide a continuous and regulated production of gas by bringing the reactants into contact in a controlled way.

lanthanide series or lanthanide metals: a series of 15 similar metallic elements between lanthanum and lutetium. They are transition metals and are also called rare earths.

latent heat: the amount of heat that is absorbed or released during the process of changing state between gas, liquid, or solid. For example, heat is absorbed when a substance melts, and it is released again when the substance solidifies.

lattice: a regular arrangement of atoms, ions, or molecules in a crystalline solid.

leaching: the extraction of a substance by percolating a solvent through a material. *Example:* when water flows through an ore, some of the heavy metals in it may be leached out causing environmental pollution.

Liebig condenser: a piece of glassware consisting of a sloping, water-cooled tube. The design allows a volatile material to be condensed and collected.

liquefaction: to make something liquid.

liquid/liquid phase: a form of matter that has a fixed volume but no fixed shape.

lime (quicklime): calcium oxide (CaO). A white, caustic solid manufactured by heating limestone and used for making mortar, fertilizer, or bleach.

limewater: an aqueous solution of calcium hydroxide used especially to detect the presence of carbon dioxide.

litmus: an indicator obtained from lichens. Used as a solution or impregnated into paper (litmus paper) that is dampened before use. Litmus turns red under acid conditions and purple in alkaline conditions. Litmus is a crude indicator when compared with Universal Indicator.

load (electronics): an impedance or circuit that receives or develops the output of a cell or other power supply.

luster: the shininess of a substance.

malleable: able to be pressed or hammered into shape.

manometer: a device for measuring gas pressure. A simple manometer is made by partly filling a U-shaped rubber tube with water and connecting one end to the source of gas whose pressure is to be measured. The pressure is always relative to atmospheric pressure.

mass: the amount of matter in an object. In everyday use the word weight is often used (somewhat incorrectly) to mean mass.

matter: anything that has mass and takes up space.

melting point: the temperature at which a substance changes state from a solid phase to a liquid phase. It is the same as freezing point.

membrane: a thin flexible sheet. A semipermeable membrane has microscopic holes of a size that will selectively allow some ions and molecules to pass through but hold others back. It thus acts as a kind of filter. *Example:* a membrane used for osmosis.

meniscus: the curved surface of a liquid that forms in a small-bore or capillary tube. The meniscus is convex (bulges upward) for mercury and is concave (sags downward) for water.

metal: a class of elements that is a good conductor of electricity and heat, has a metallic luster, is malleable and ductile, forms cations, and has oxides that are bases. Metals are formed as cations held together by a sea of electrons. A metal may also be an alloy of these elements. *Example:* sodium, calcium, gold. *See:* alloy, metalloid, nonmetal.

metallic bonding: cations reside in a "sea" of mobile electrons. It allows metals to be good conductors and means that they are not brittle. *See:* bonding.

metallic luster: *See:* luster.

metalloid: a class of elements intermediate in properties between metals and nonmetals. Metalloids are also called semimetals or semiconductors. *Example:* silicon, germanium, antimony. *See:* metal, nonmetal, semiconductor.

micronutrient: an element that the body requires in small amounts. Another term is trace element.

mineral: a solid substance made of just one element or compound. *Example:* calcite is a mineral because it consists only of calcium carbonate; halite is a mineral because it contains only sodium chloride.

mineral acid: an acid that does not contain carbon and which attacks minerals. Hydrochloric, sulfuric, and nitric acids are the main mineral acids.

miscible: capable of being mixed.

mixing combustion: the form of combustion that occurs when two gases thoroughly mix before they ignite and so produce almost complete combustion. *Example:* when a Bunsen flame is blue.

mixture: a material that can be separated into two or more substances using physical means. *Example:* a mixture of copper(II) sulfate and cadmium sulfide can be separated by filtration.

molar mass: the mass per mole of atoms of an element. It has the same value and uses the same units as atomic weight. *Example:* molar mass of chlorine is 35.45 g/mol. *See:* atomic weight.

mole: 1 mole is the amount of a substance that contains Avagadro's number (6×10^{23}) of particles. *Example:* 1 mole of carbon-12 weighs exactly 12 g.

molecular mass: *See:* molar mass.

molecular weight: *See:* molar mass.

molecule: a group of two or more atoms held together by chemical bonds. *Example:* O_2.

monoclinic system: a grouping of crystals that look like double-ended chisel blades.

monomer: a small molecule and building block for larger chain molecules or polymers ("mono"

means one, "mer" means part). *Examples:* tetrafluoroethene for teflon, ethene for polyethene.

native element: an element that occurs in an uncombined state. *Examples:* sulfur, gold.

native metal: a pure form of a metal, not combined as a compound. Native metal is more common in poorly reactive elements than in those that are very reactive. *Examples:* copper, gold.

net ionic reaction: the overall, or net, change that occurs in a reaction, seen in terms of ions.

neutralization: the reaction of acids and bases to produce a salt and water. The reaction causes hydrogen from the acid and hydroxide from the base to be changed to water. *Example:* hydrochloric acid reacts with, and neutralizes, sodium hydroxide to form the salt sodium chloride (common salt) and water. The term is more generally used for any reaction in which the pH changes toward 7.0, which is the pH of a neutral solution. *See:* pH.

neutralization point: *See:* end point.

neutron: a particle inside the nucleus of an atom that is neutral and has no charge.

newton (N): the unit of force required to give one kilogram an acceleration of one meter per second every second ($1\ ms^{-2}$).

nitrate: a compound that includes nitrogen and oxygen and contains more oxygen than a nitrite. Nitrate ions have the chemical formula NO_3^-. *Examples:* sodium nitrate $NaNO_3$ and lead nitrate $Pb(NO_3)_2$.

nitrite: a compound that includes nitrogen and oxygen and contains less oxygen than a nitrate. Nitrite ions have the chemical formula NO_2^-. *Example:* sodium nitrite $NaNO_2$.

noble gases: the members of Group 8 of the Periodic Table: helium, neon, argon, krypton, xenon, radon. These gases are almost entirely unreactive.

noble metals: silver, gold, platinum, and mercury. These are the least reactive metals.

noncombustible: a substance that will not combust or burn. *Example:* carbon dioxide.

nonmetal: a brittle substance that does not conduct electricity. *Examples:* sulfur, phosphorus, all gases. *See:* metal, metalloid.

normal salt: salts that do not contain a hydroxide (OH⁻) ion, which would make them basic salts, or a hydrogen ion, which would make them acid salts. *Example:* sodium chloride (NaCl).

nucleus: the small, positively charged particle at the center of an atom. The nucleus is responsible for most of the mass of an atom.

opaque: a substance that will not transmit light so that it is impossible to see through it. Most solids are opaque.

ore: a rock containing enough of a useful substance to make mining it worthwhile. *Example:* bauxite, aluminum ore.

organic acid: an acid containing carbon and hydrogen. *Example:* methanoic (formic) acid (HCOOH).

organic chemistry: the study of organic compounds.

organic compound (organic substance; organic material): a compound (or substance) that contains carbon and usually hydrogen. (The carbonates are usually excluded.) *Examples:* methane (CH_4), chloromethane (CH_3Cl), ethene (C_2H_4), ethanol (C_2H_5OH), ethanoic acid (C_2H_3OOH) etc.

organic solvent: an organic substance that will dissolve other substances. *Example:* carbon tetrachloride (CCl_4).

osmosis: a process whereby molecules of a liquid solvent move through a semipermeable membrane from a region of low concentration of a solute to a region with a high concentration of a solute.

oxidation-reduction reaction (redox reaction): reaction in which oxidation and reduction occurs; a reaction in which electrons are transferred. *Example:* copper and oxygen react to produce copper(II) oxide. The copper is oxidized, and oxygen is reduced.

oxidation: combination with oxygen or a reaction in which an atom, ion, or molecule loses electrons to an oxidizing agent. (Note that an oxidizing agent does not have to contain oxygen.) The opposite of oxidation is reduction. *See:* reduction.

oxidation number (oxidation state): the effective charge on an atom in a compound. An increase in oxidation number corresponds to oxidation, and a decrease to reduction. Shown in Roman numerals. *Example:* manganate(IV).

oxidation state: *See:* oxidation number.

oxide: a compound that includes oxygen and one other element. *Example:* copper oxide (CuO).

oxidize: to combine with or gain oxygen or to react such that an atom, ion, or molecule loses electrons to an oxidizing agent.

oxidizing agent: a substance that removes electrons from another substance being oxidized (and therefore is itself reduced) in a redox reaction. *Example:* chlorine (Cl_2).

ozone: a form of oxygen whose molecules contain three atoms of oxygen. Ozone is regarded as a beneficial gas when high in the atmosphere because it blocks ultraviolet rays. It is a harmful gas when breathed in, so low-level ozone that is produced as part of city smog is regarded as a form of pollution. The ozone layer is the uppermost part of the stratosphere.

partial pressure: the pressure a gas in a mixture would exert if it alone occupied a flask. *Example:* oxygen makes up about a fifth of the atmosphere. Its partial pressure is therefore about a fifth of normal atmospheric pressure.

pascal: the unit of pressure, equal to one newton per square meter of surface. *See:* newton.

patina: a surface coating that develops on metals and protects them from further corrosion. *Example:* the green coating on copper carbonate that forms on copper statues.

percolate: to move slowly through the pores of a rock.

period: a row in the Periodic Table.

Periodic Table: a chart organizing elements by atomic number and chemical properties into groups and periods.

pestle and mortar: a pestle is a ceramic rod with a rounded end; a mortar is a ceramic dish. Pestle and mortar are used together to pound or grind solids into fine powders.

Petri dish: a shallow glass or plastic dish with a lid.

petroleum: a natural mixture of a range of gases, liquids, and solids derived from the decomposed remains of plants and animals.

pH: a measure of the hydrogen ion concentration in a liquid. Neutral is pH 7.0; numbers greater than this are alkaline; smaller numbers are acidic. *See:* neutralization, acid, base.

pH meter: a device that accurately measures the pH of a solution. A

pH meter is a voltmeter that measures the electric potential difference between two electrodes (which are attached to the meter through a probe) when they are submerged in a solution. The readings are shown on a dial or digital display.

phase: a particular state of matter. A substance may exist as a solid, liquid, or gas and may change between these phases with addition or removal of energy. *Examples:* ice, liquid, and vapor are the three phases of water. Ice undergoes a phase change to water when heat energy is added.

phosphor: any material that glows when energized by ultraviolet or electron beams such as in fluorescent tubes and cathode ray tubes. Phosphors, such as phosphorus, emit light after the source of excitation is cut off. This is why they glow in the dark. By contrast, fluorescors, such as fluorite, only emit light while they are being excited by ultraviolet light or an electron beam.

photochemical smog: photochemical reactions are caused by the energy of sunlight. Photochemical smog is a mixture of tiny particles and a brown haze caused by the reaction of colorless nitric oxide from vehicle exhausts and oxygen of the air to form brown nitrogen dioxide.

photon: a parcel of light energy.

photosynthesis: the process by which plants use the energy of the Sun to make the compounds they need for life. In photosynthesis six molecules of carbon dioxide from the air combine with six molecules of water, forming one molecule of glucose (sugar) and releasing six molecules of oxygen back into the atmosphere.

pipe-clay triangle: a device made from three small pieces of ceramic tube that are wired together in the shape of a triangle. Pipe-clay

triangles are used to support round-bottomed dishes when they are heated in a Bunsen flame.

pipette: a log, slender glass tube used, in conjunction with a pipette filler, to draw up and then transfer accurately measured amounts of liquid.

plastic: (material) a carbon-based substance consisting of long chains (polymers) of simple molecules. The word plastic is commonly restricted to synthetic polymers. *Examples:* polyvinyl chloride, nylon: **(property)** a material is plastic if it can be made to change shape easily. Plastic materials will remain in the new shape. (Compare with elastic, a property whereby a material goes back to its original shape.)

pneumatic trough: a shallow water-filled glass dish used to house a beehive shelf and a gas jar as part of the apparatus for collecting a gas over water.

polar solvent: a solvent in which the atoms have partial electric charges. *Example:* water.

polymer: a compound that is made of long chains by combining molecules (called monomers) as repeating units. ("Poly" means many, "mer" means part.) *Examples:* polytetrafluoroethene or Teflon from tetrafluoroethene, Terylene from terephthalic acid and ethane-1,2-diol (ethylene glycol).

polymerization: a chemical reaction in which large numbers of similar molecules arrange themselves into large molecules, usually long chains. This process usually happens when there is a suitable catalyst present. *Example:* ethene gas reacts to form polyethene in the presence of certain catalysts.

polymorphism: (meaning many shapes) the tendency of some materials to have more than one solid form. *Example:* carbon as diamond, graphite and buckminsterfullerene.

porous: a material containing many small holes or cracks. Quite often the pores are connected, and liquids, such as water or oil, can move through them.

potential difference: a measure of the work that must be done to move an electric charge from one point to the other in a circuit. Potential difference is measured in volts, V. *See:* electrical potential.

precious metal: silver, gold, platinum, iridium and palladium. Each is prized for its rarity.

precipitate: a solid substance formed as a result of a chemical reaction between two liquids or gases. *Example:* iron (III) hydroxide is precipitated when sodium hydroxide solution is added to iron (III) chloride. *See:* gelatinous precipitate, granular precipitate.

preservative: a substance that prevents the natural organic decay processes from occurring. Many substances can be used safely for this purpose, including sulfites and nitrogen gas.

pressure: the force per unit area measured in pascals. *See:* pascal.

product: a substance produced by a chemical reaction. *Example:* when the reactants copper and oxygen react, they produce the product copper oxide.

proton: a positively charged particle in the nucleus of an atom that balances out the charge of the surrounding electrons.

proton number: this is the modern expression for atomic number. *See:* atomic number.

purify: to remove all impurities from a mixture, perhaps by precipitation or filtration.

pyrolysis: chemical decomposition brought about by heat. *Example:* decomposition of lead nitrate. *See:* destructive distillation.

pyrometallurgy: refining a metal from its ore using heat. A blast furnace or smelter is the main equipment used.

quantitative: measurement of the amounts of constituents of a substance, for example, by mass or volume. *See:* gravimetric analysis, volumetric analysis.

radiation: the exchange of energy with the surroundings through the transmission of waves or particles of energy. Radiation is a form of energy transfer that can happen through space; no intervening medium is required (as would be the case for conduction and convection).

radical: an atom, molecule, or ion with at least one unpaired electron. *Example:* nitrogen monoxide (NO).

radioactive: emitting radiation or particles from the nucleus of its atoms.

radioactive decay: a change in a radioactive element due to loss of mass through radiation. For example, uranium decays (changes) to lead.

reactant: a starting material that takes part in and undergoes change during a chemical reaction. *Example:* hydrochloric acid and calcium carbonate are reactants; the reaction produces the products calcium chloride, carbon dioxide, and water.

reaction: the recombination of two substances using parts of each substance to produce new substances. *Example:* the reactants sodium chloride and sulfuric acid react and recombine to form the products sodium sulfate, chlorine, and water.

reactivity: the tendency of a substance to react with other substances. The term is most widely used in comparing the reactivity of metals. Metals are arranged in a reactivity series.

reactivity series: the series of metals organized in order of their reactivity, with the most reactive metals, such as sodium, at the top and the least react metals, such as gold, at the bottom. Hydrogen is usually included in the series for comparative purposes.

reagent: a commonly available substance (reactant) used to create a reaction. Reagents are the chemicals normally kept on chemistry laboratory shelf. Many substances called reagents are most commonly used for test purposes.

redox reaction (oxidation-reduction reaction): a reaction that involves oxidation and reduction; a reactions in which electrons are transferred. *See:* oxidation-reduction.

reducing agent: a substance that gives electrons to another substance being reduced (and therefore itself being oxidized) in a redox reaction. *Example:* hydrogen sulfide (H_2S).

reduction: the removal of oxygen from, or the addition of hydrogen to, a compound. Also a reaction in which an atom, ion, or molecule gains electrons from a reducing agent. (The opposite of reduction is oxidation.)

reduction tube: a boiling tube with a small hole near the closed end. The tube is mounted horizontally, a sample is placed in the tube, and a reducing gas, such as carbon monoxide, is passed through the tube. The oxidized gas escapes through the small hole.

refining: separating a mixture into the simpler substances of which it is made.

reflux distillation system: a form of distillation using a Liebig condenser placed vertically, so that all the vapors created during boiling are condensed back into the liquid rather than escaping. In this way the concentration of all the reactants remains constant.

relative atomic mass: in the past a measure of the mass of an atom on a scale relative to the mass of an atom of hydrogen, where hydrogen is 1. Nowadays a measure of the mass of an atom relative to the mass of one twelfth of an atom of carbon-12. If the relative atomic mass is given as a rounded figure, it is called an approximate relative atomic mass. *Examples*: chlorine 35, calcium 40, gold 197. *See:* atomic mass, atomic weight.

reversible reaction: a reaction in which the products can be transformed back into their original chemical form. *Example:* heated iron reacts with steam to produce iron oxide and hydrogen. If the hydrogen is passed over this heated oxide it forms iron and steam. $3Fe + 4H_2O \rightleftharpoons Fe_3O_4 + 4H_2$.

roast: heating a substance for a long time at a high temperature, as in a furnace.

rust: the product of the corrosion of iron and steel in the presence of air and water.

salt: a compound, often involving a metal, that is the reaction product of an acid and a base, or of two elements. (Note "salt" is also the common word for sodium chloride, common salt, or table salt.) *Example:* sodium chloride (NaCl) and potassium sulfate (K_2SO_4) *See:* acid salt, basic salt, normal salt.

salt bridge: a permeable material soaked in a salt solution that allows ions to be transferred from one container to another. The salt solution remains unchanged during this transfer. *Example:* sodium sulfate used as a salt bridge in a galvanic cell.

saponification: a reaction between a fat and a base that produces a soap.

saturated: a state in which a liquid can hold no more of a substance. If any more of the substance is added, it will not dissolve.

saturated hydrocarbon: a hydrocarbon in which the carbon atoms are held with single bonds. *Example:* ethane (C_2H_4).

saturated solution: a solution that holds the maximum possible amount of dissolved material. When saturated, the rate of dissolving solid and that of recrystallization solid are the same, and a condition of equilibrium is reached. The amount of material in solution varies with the temperature; cold solutions can hold less dissolved solid material than hot solutions. Gases are more soluble in cold liquids than hot liquids.

sediment: material that settles out at the bottom of a liquid when it is still. A precipitate is one form of sediment.

semiconductor: a material of intermediate conductivity. Semiconductor devices often use silicon when they are made as part of diodes, transistors, or integrated circuits. Elements intermediate between metals and nonmetals are also sometimes called semiconductors. *Example:* germanium oxide, germanium. *See:* metalloid.

semipermeable membrane: a thin material that acts as a fine sieve or filter, allowing small molecules to pass, but holding large molecules back.

separating column: used in chromatography. A tall glass tube containing a porous disc near the base and filled with a substance (for example, aluminum oxide, which is known as a stationary phase) that can adsorb materials on its surface. When a mixture is passed through the column, fractions are retarded by differing amounts, so that each fraction is washed through the column in sequence.

separating funnel: a pear-shaped glassware funnel designed to permit the separation of immiscible liquids by simply pouring off the more dense liquid while leaving the less dense liquid in the funnel.

series circuit: an electrical circuit in which all of the components are joined end to end in a line.

shell: the term used to describe the imaginary ball-shaped surface outside the nucleus of an atom that would be formed by a set of electrons of similar energy. The outermost shell is known as the valence shell. *Example:* neon has shells containing 2 and 8 electrons.

side-arm boiling tube: a boiling tube with an integral glass pipe near its open end. The side arm is normally used for the entry or exit of a gas.

simple distillation: the distillation of a substance when only one volatile fraction is to be collected. Simple distillation uses a Liebig condenser arranged almost horizontally. When the liquid mixture is heated and vapors are produced, they enter the condenser and then flow away from the flask and can be collected. *Example:* simple distillation of ethanoic acid.

slag: a mixture of substances that are waste products of a furnace. Most slags are composed mainly of silicates.

smelting: roasting a substance in order to extract the metal contained in it.

smog: a mixture of smoke and fog. The term is used to describe city fogs in which there is a large proportion of particulate matter (tiny pieces of carbon from exhausts) and also a high concentration of sulfur and nitrogen gases and probably ozone. *See:* photochemical smog.

smokeless fuel: a fuel that has been subjected to partial pyrolysis so that there is no more loose particulate matter remaining. *Example:* Coke is a smokeless fuel.

solid/solid phase: a rigid form of matter that maintains its shape whatever its container.

solubility: the maximum amount of a substance that can be contained in a solvent.

soluble: readily dissolvable in a solvent.

solute: a substance that has dissolved. *Example:* sodium chloride in water.

solution: a mixture of a liquid (the solvent) and at least one other substance of lesser abundance (the solute). Mixtures can be separated by physical means, for example, by evaporation and cooling. *See:* aqueous solution.

solvent: the main substance in a solution.

spectator ions: the ionic part of a compound that does not play an active part in a reaction. *Example:* when magnesium ribbon is placed in copper(II) sulfate solution the copper is displaced from the solution by the magnesium while the sulfate ion (SO_4^{2-}) plays no part in the reaction and so behaves as a spectator ion.

spectrum: the range of colors that make up visible light (as seen in a rainbow) or across all electromagnetic radiation, arranged in progression according to their wavelength.

spontaneous combustion: the effect of a very reactive material or combination of reactants that suddenly reach their ignition temperature and begin to combust rapidly.

standard temperature and pressure (STP): 0°C at one atmosphere (a pressure that supports a column of mercury 760 mm high). Also given as 0°C at 100 kilopascals. *See:* atmospheric pressure.

state of matter: the physical form of matter. There are three states of matter: liquid, solid, and gaseous.

stationary phase: a name given to a material that is used as a medium for separating a liquid mixture, as in in chromatography.

strong acid: an acid that has completely dissociated (ionized) in water. Mineral acids are strong acids.

sublime/sublimation: the change of a substance from solid to gas, or vice versa, without going through a liquid phase. *Example:* iodine sublimes from a purple solid to a purple gas.

substance: a type of material, including mixtures.

sulfate: a compound that includes sulfur and oxygen and contains more oxygen than a sulfite. Sulfate ions have the chemical formula SO_4^{2-}. *Examples:* calcium sulfate $CaSO_4$ (the main constituent of gypsum) and aluminum sulfate $Al_2(SO_4)_3$ (an alum).

sulfide: a sulfur compound that contains no oxygen. Sulfide ions have the chemical formula S^{2-}. *Example:* hydrogen sulfide (H_2S).

sulfite: a compound that includes sulfur and oxygen but contains less oxygen than a sulfate. Sulfite ions have the chemical formula SO_3^{2-}. *Example:* sodium sulfite Na_2SO_3.

supercooling: the ability of some substances to cool below their normal freezing point. *Example:* sodium thiosulfate.

supersaturated solution: a solution in which the amount of solute is greater than what would normally be expected in a saturated solution. Most solids are more soluble in hot solutions than in cold. If a hot saturated solution is made up, the solution can be rapidly cooled down below its freezing point before it begins to solidify. This is a supersaturated solution.

surface tension: the force that operates on the surface of a liquid and that makes it act as though it were covered with an invisible, elastic film.

suspension: a mist of tiny particles in a liquid.

synthesis: a reaction in which a substance is formed from simpler reactants. *Example:* hydrogen gas and chlorine gas react to sythesize hydrogen chloride gas. The term can also be applied to polymerization of organic compounds.

synthetic: does not occur naturally but has to be manufactured. Commonly used in the name "synthetic fiber."

tare: an allowance made for the weight of a container.

tarnish: a coating that develops as a result of the reaction between a metal and substances in the air. The most common form of tarnishing is a very thin transparent oxide coating.

terminal: one of the electrodes of a battery.

test (chemical): a reagent or a procedure used to reveal the presence of another reagent. *Example:* litmus and other indicators are used to test the acidity or alkalinity of a substance.

test tube: A thin glass tube closed at one end and used for chemical tests, etc. The composition and thickness of the glass is such that while it is inert to most chemical reactions, it may not sustain very high temperatures but can usually be heated in a Bunsen flame. *See:* boiling tube.

thermal decomposition: the breakdown of a substance using heat: *See* pyrolysis.

thermoplastic: a plastic that will soften and can repeatedly be molded into shape on heating and will set into the molded shape as it cools.

thermoset: a plastic that will set into a molded shape as it cools, but which cannot be made soft by reheating.

thistle funnel: a narrow tube, expanded at the top into a thistlehead-shaped vessel. It is used as a funnel when introducing small amounts of liquid reactant. When fitted with a tap, it can be used to control the rate of entry of a reactant. *See:* burette.

titration: the analysis of the composition of a substance in a solution by measuring the volume of that solution (the titrant, normally in a burette) needed to react with a given volume of another solution (the titrate, normally placed in a flask). An indicator is often used to signal change. *Example:* neutralization of sodium hydroxide using hydrochloric acid in an acid–base titration. *See:* end point.

toxic: poisonous.

transition metals: the group of metals that belong to the d-block of the Periodic Table. Transition metals commonly have a number of differently colored oxidation states. *Examples:* iron, vanadium.

Universal Indicator: a mixture of indicators commonly used in the laboratory because of its reliability. Used as a solution or impregnated into paper (Indicator paper) that is dampened before use. Universal Indicator changes color from purple in a strongly alkaline solution through green when the solution is neutral to red in strongly acidic solutions. Universal Indicator is more accurate than litmus paper but less accurate than a pH meter.

unsaturated hydrocarbon: a hydrocarbon in which at least one bond is a double or triple bond. Hydrogen atoms can be added to unsaturated compounds to form saturated compounds. *Example:* ethene, C_2H_4 or $CH_2=CH_2$.

vacuum: a container from which air has been removed using a pump.

valency: the number of bonds that an atom can form. *Examples:* calcium has a valency of 2 and bromine a valency of 1

valency shell: the outermost shell of an atom. *See:* shell.

vapor: the gaseous phase of a substance. *See:* gas.

vein: a fissure in rock that has filled with ore or other mineral-bearing rock.

viscous: slow-moving, syrupy. A liquid that has a low viscosity is said to be mobile.

volatile: readily forms a gas.

volatile fraction: the part of a liquid mixture that will readily vaporize under the conditions prevailing during the reaction. *See:* fraction, vapor.

water of crystallization: the water molecules absorbed into the crystalline structure as a liquid changes to a solid. *Example:* hydrated copper(II) sulfate $CuSO_4 \bullet 5H_2O$. *See:* hydrate.

weak acid and **weak base**: an acid or base that has only partly dissociated (ionized) in water. Most organic acids are weak acids. *See:* organic acid.

weight: the gravitational force on a substance. *See:* mass.

X-rays: a form of very short wave radiation.

MASTER INDEX